SPEAK LIFE

WORDS
THAT WORK
WONDERS

E. W. KENYON AND
DON GOSSETT

WHITAKER
HOUSE

SPEAK LIFE:
WORDS THAT WORK WONDERS

ISBN: 978-1-62911-914-4
eBook ISBN: 978-1-60374-909-1
Printed in the United States of America
© 2016 by Debra Gossett

Don Gossett Ministries
P.O. Box 2
Blaine, WA 98231
www.dongossett.com

Kenyon's Gospel Publishing Society
P.O. Box 973
Lynnwood, WA 98046
www.kenyons.org

Whitaker House
1030 Hunt Valley Circle
New Kensington, PA 15068
www.whitakerhouse.com

This book has been printed digitally and produced in a standard specification in order to ensure its continuing availability.

CONTENTS

PARK III: WORDS THAT BRING HEALING

PART IV: WORDS THAT BRING VICTORY

FOREWORD

The word *confession*, in its positive biblical meaning, means affirming what God has said in His Word. It is witnessing to the Word's declaration. It is testifying to truths revealed in the Bible.

We have been divinely instructed to *"hold fast our profession"* (Hebrews 4:14). The writer of the book of Hebrews further stated, *"Let us hold fast the profession of our faith without wavering; (for he is faithful that promised;)"* (Hebrews 10:23). Not only are we to *"hold fast"* our confession of the Word, but we are also to affirm constantly those things that God has revealed to us. (See Titus 3:8.)

Confession is saying what God has said in His Word about a certain thing. It is agreeing with God. It is saying the same thing the Scripture says. To hold fast your confession is to say what God has said over and over until the thing desired in your heart and promised in the Word is fully manifested. There is no such thing as possession without confession.

When we discover our rights in Christ, we are to affirm these things constantly. Testify to them. Witness to these tremendous Bible facts. The apostle Paul said, *"That the communication of thy faith may become effectual by the acknowledging of every good thing which is in you in Christ Jesus"* (Philemon 1:6).

Affirmations of truth should ring from our lips constantly. We are to hold fast to them without wavering. The penalty for wavering in our confession is that we deny ourselves God's promise and the performance of it. *"But let him ask in faith, nothing wavering. For he that wavereth is like a wave of the sea driven with the wind and tossed. For let not that man think that he shall receive any thing of the Lord"* (James 1:6–7).

The psalmist said, *"Let the redeemed of the LORD say so"* (Psalm 107:2), and again, *"Let such as love thy salvation say continually, let God be magnified"* (Psalm 70:4).

But more than truth, Scripture is full of life itself. Jesus said, *"He that heareth my word, and believeth on him that sent me, **hath everlasting life**"* (John 5:24). He also said, *"It is the spirit that quickeneth; the flesh profiteth* *nothing: the words that I speak unto you, they are spirit, and **they are life***" (John 6:63.)

The Word of God is life itself. When we confess it, we *Speak Life* into our lives and into the lives of others around us. And that life is the "abundant life" that Jesus spoke about, lives filled with success, healing, power, and every good thing.

Through the Word of God, you and I have the distinct privilege of being able to *Speak Life*, each and every day. But to do so, we must constantly return to His Word to be refilled. As the apostle Peter said, "*Lord, to whom shall we go? thou hast the words of eternal life*" (John 6:68).

In this book, I have included many teachings from the works of Dr. E. W. Kenyon along with messages of my own, all on the power of confessing God's Word. I pray that they will stir you to get the Word of God deep into your heart so that it will flow back out to the world in the words you speak.

—*Don Gossett*

PART I:
WORDS THAT BRING SUCCESS

DON GOSSETT

SPEAK SUCCESS, NOT FAILURE

Speak as a new creation, not the old creation filled with envy and rottenness. Declare it:

> [I am] *a new creature: old things are passed away; behold, all things are become new.* (2 Corinthians 5:17)

Speak your righteousness in Christ, not unworthiness. Affirm it:

> [I am] *the righteousness of God in* [Jesus Christ].
> (2 Corinthians 5:21)

Speak the language of the new kingdom of God's dear Son in which you now dwell, not the old kingdom of darkness from which you have been translated.

> *Giving thanks unto the Father, which hath made us meet to be partakers of the inheritance of the saints in light: Who hath delivered us from the power of darkness, and hath translated us into the kingdom of his dear Son: in whom we have redemption through his blood, even the forgiveness of sins.* (Colossians 1:12–14)

Speak that you are an heir of God and a joint heir with Jesus Christ, not your old identification as a captive to sin and Satan. Testify to it:

> I have a rich inheritance. I am blessed with every spiritual blessing. The Father Himself loveth me.

Speak that you have the life of God in your mortal body, not the old spirit of inferiority, failure, and frustration.

> *In him we live, and move, and have our being.* (Acts 17:28)

Speak healing and health, not how sick and diseased you are. Isaiah 33:24 foretells a future time when *"the inhabitant shall not say, I am sick."* That's a good practice in kingdom living now. Don't say. "I am sick," but speak the Word that heals. *"With his stripes we are healed"* (Isaiah 53:5).

Speak financial success, not poverty and misery.

Speak marriage success, not marriage failure.

Then thou shalt make thy way prosperous, and then thou shalt have good success. (Joshua 1:8)

E. W. KENYON

FOR A MESS OF POTTAGE

Esau sold his birthright. Had he not done it, the Scriptures would have read, "The God of Abraham, the God of Isaac, the God of Esau." Now it reads, "*The God of Jacob.*"

Esau was the oldest, and so the birthright belonged to him. If Esau had not sold his birthright for a mess of pottage, Jesus would have come through his genealogy rather than Jacob's.

That pottage was named Edom. So Esau was known as Edom—a name of derision, shame, and failure.

Many people today are selling their birthright for a moment's pleasure. They are bartering their birthright to hold the opinion of some person. They are selling their birthright for the pleasures of a moment.

How Esau wept when he realized what he had done. But his tears and regret did not bring back the thing that he had bartered away.

Many sell their future happiness for an evening of pleasure. They sell success and future independence for an hour of pleasure. They sell their birthright of fellowship with heaven for a mess of pottage. The price that they received perished with the using. They sold their power with God, their right to use the name of Jesus, the fullness of blessing, for a mess of pottage! Remember that Esau's pleasure died when he ate. And so will ours. The pleasure will leave a pain. The pleasure will leave a bad taste in the mouth of memory.

You have everything. Don't throw it all away. The Spirit is calling on you to cut it out, to turn back again to Him. Ask for His forgiveness, knowing that if you confess your sins, He is faithful and righteous to forgive you and cleanse you from all unrighteousness. (See John 3:16.) Then, as He has forgotten our blunders, so we can forget them and set our face toward Him, going out and winning our place in the world.

Study the Word; give yourself to it. Go out after lost men and women. Talk Jesus; preach Jesus; live Jesus; live with His reality throbbing through you. Take Him into your life. Yield to His lordship.

None of us know the vast issues tied up in our lives. In our hands now may be the destiny of nations. Your voice may become not only a local voice but a national voice. We cannot stop believing in our birthright in Christ. The mess of pottage is not worth it. Remember that there is no value in good impulses that die unborn. Translate the impulse into an action, confession, and life.

DON GOSSETT

WORDS THAT
WORK WONDERS

If only we would realize the power in our words, how different our lives would be. It has been said that "the pen is mightier than the sword." How much mightier are the words of our pen and of our mouth when our words are the Word of God. *"Whoso offereth praise glorifieth me: and to him that ordereth his conversation aright will I show the salvation of God"* (Psalm 50:23). Some words that can work wonders are:

Words of Praise. *"I will bless the LORD at all times: his praise shall continually be in my mouth"* (Psalm 34:1). Resolve to be a bold "praiser" from now on. As a "praiser," extol the Lord not so much for His gifts which you receive but to magnify the wonderful Giver Himself.

Words of Edification and Grace. Resolve to *"ordereth his conversation aright"* (Psalm 50:23), that *"no corrupt communication proceed out of your mouth, but that which is good to the use of edifying, that it may minister grace unto the hearers"* (Ephesians 4:29).

Words of Bold Authority Overcoming Satan's Power. *"They overcame him by the blood of the Lamb, and by the word of their testimony"* (Revelation 12:11).

Words of Confession of God's Word. Confession always precedes possession. The word "confession" means "to say the same thing." Dare to say exactly what God says in His Word. Agree with God by speaking His Word in all circumstances.

When we *"ordereth [our] conversation[s] aright,"* God manifests the benefits of His great salvation. *"With the mouth confession is made unto salvation"* (Romans 10:10). And remember that, when we make confession unto salvation, it includes healing, deliverance, and every spiritual and physical blessing provided for us in Christ's atonement.

As confession always precedes possession, so a wrong confession, or a negative confession, precedes the possession of wrong things. Your tongue, used wrongly, can cause you much trouble. *"Whoso keepeth his mouth and his tongue keepeth his soul from troubles"* (Proverbs 21:23). *"Thou art snared with the words of thy mouth, thou art taken with the words of thy mouth"* (Proverbs 6:2). Refuse to have a wrong confession.

Remember that your words can work wonders. Therefore, speak words of praise, words of singing, words of faith in God's Word, words of bold authority expelling Satan's power. Truly, words are the "coin of the kingdom," and you can boldly speak words that will work wonders for you!

E. W. KENYON
THE SECRET OF SUCCESS

I have been trying to help a young man for a long time, but I never could get him to come to the point of making an unqualified committal of himself, his ambitions, and his future to the lordship of Jesus. He would almost do it.

He would confess Christ as his Savior, but he never would go the whole length. But today he saw it. The gloom and indecision faded in the bright light of a new joy. I am certain that the lordship of Jesus solves every problems of life. When we really reach the place where we will put the crown upon the head of the man of Galilee and say, "Master you rule from today," then you can say, "*The* LORD *is my shepherd; I shall not want*" (Psalm 23:1). What a blessing that is. You shall not want for money; you shall not want for anything.

The Lord is my Shepherd, I cannot fail. Not only can you say, "*I shall not want*," but you know that He has blessed you with every spiritual blessing in the heavenlies in Christ; and every blessing that belongs to the plan of redemption automatically becomes yours the moment you confess His lordship.

The lordship of Christ means the lordship of the Word. That solves every problem because the Word covers every issue of life. The Word is final to you. "My God shall supply every need of yours." (See Philippians 4:19.)

You stop worrying. All is thanksgiving now. You are out of the wilderness, out of the fear and bondage of the yesterdays and tomorrows. He is now the protector of your life. If He says He is the strength of your life, then you know that your body is strong enough to do anything that He wishes.

You are no longer fearful. You are not afraid of diseases or weakness or sickness or lack of ability, for He has become your strength. He is your ability for every emergency. What a burden rolls from the heart when Jesus Christ becomes your ability. Now you can say, "I have ability for anything. I have strength to do anything He wishes."

"*I can do all things in* [Him] *who strengthens me*" (Philippians 4:13 NKJV). What a fearless outlook this is. The lordship of Jesus means the lordship of Love. "*The love of God is shed abroad in our hearts by the Holy Ghost*" (Romans 5:5). The old bitterness and hardness leaves the voice and the eyes.

You walk in love. You are not afraid of any temptation, any situation, or any trial, for your Lord is at hand. That means that you have a protector, a shield. No disease can lay hold upon your body. You have passed out of the realm of weakness and failure, into the realm of strength and victory.

He has become your Righteousness, so that now you and your Savior can stand together before the Father without fear. Prayer becomes a joy, because Jesus is your Lord, and your Lord has said, "Whatsoever you ask of the Father in my name, He will do it." (See John 14:13.) Your Lord is looking after that end of your prayer life. He represents you at the throne. He upholds you. He is your Intercessor. He ever lives to make intercession for you. If you get into any kind of trouble, He is your Lawyer, your righteous Advocate.

What a fearless victorious life is ahead of you. This is the genius of life. Here is the secret of the whole thing: The moment He becomes your Lord, you become independent of circumstances. Do you remember how independent He was when He wanted to meet the disciples one night and they were in the midst of the seas in a storm? That did not bother Him. He walked out and met them. He quieted the sea. He was Master; He is Master; that One is your Lord. That One who fed the multitude, who healed the sick and raised the dead, is your Lord.

DON GOSSETT

YOU ARE GOD'S CHILD

Psychologists have long been talking about the "inferiority complex."

As a born-again Christian, you are in Christ and Christ is in you. The very word "Christian" means we are "Christ-in" people. We're not "Christian workers." We are "Christ containers."

There can be absolutely nothing inferior about you because there is nothing inferior about Christ—and you contain Him. Sixty-seven different times in the writings of Paul alone, we are told that we are *in Christ* if we are born again.

How can you be inferior when *"ye are dead, and your life is hid with Christ in God"* (Colossians 3:3)?

If you were a king's son, or a king's daughter, would you feel inferior? Yet you are a child of the King of Kings! How can you feel inferior when you are the apple of God's eye, and He created everything there is?

You may feel that you are insufficient in some area, and—in the natural—you may be right. But the Word of God says *"our sufficiency is of God"* (2 Corinthians 3:5). You need not worry about what you can or cannot do, for God *in you* can do everything!

Christianity is a "say-so" way of life. Psalm 107:2 says, *"Let the redeemed of the* LORD *say so"*! This is how you became a Christian in the first place: *"With the mouth confession is made unto salvation"* (Romans 10:10). Your mouth makes confession *"unto salvation,"* not only when you are born again, but also whenever you operate according to Mark 11:23–24:

> For verily I say unto you, That whosoever shall say unto this mountain, Be thou removed, and be thou cast into the sea; and shall not doubt in his heart, but shall believe that those things which he saith shall come to pass; he shall have whatsoever he saith. Therefore I say unto you, What things soever ye desire, when ye pray, believe that ye receive them, and ye shall have them.

You cannot rise higher that your confession. A wrong confession will imprison you; a right confession will set you free.

What are we to say? Again and again, I repeat that we should say what God says, for God's Word is truth. It doesn't matter what we think, feel, or see; what does matter is what God has told us in His Word.

Joel 3:10 says, *"Let the weak say, I am strong."* Therefore, confess that you are strong—whether you feel strong or not. Say, "In obedience to Joel 3:10, I say I'm strong."

What is the area in which the devil would try to weaken you? Do you feel defeated? Say, *"Now thanks be unto God, which always causeth us to triumph in Christ"* (2 Corinthians 2:14). Do you feel apologetic? Say, *"I know whom I have believed, and am persuaded that he is able to keep that which I have committed unto him against that day"* (2 Timothy 1:12). Do you feel timid? Say, *"If God be for us, who can be against us?"* (Romans 8:31).

As you allow Christ to live His life in you, you can overcome your inferiority complex by a joyful awareness that it is *"not I, but Christ [who] liveth in me"* (Galatians 2:20).

SUCCESS IS WITHIN YOUR REACH

Success is a God-made thing, available to every one of His children. There is no need for failure and no place for it in the purposes of God. There is strength for your physical body and for your mind. He is the strength of your life. That includes the whole man: strength of will, strength of mind, strength of body.

You have no right to be a weakling in the presence of God, who has offered His ability to you.

> And such trust have we through Christ to God-ward: not that we are sufficient of ourselves to think any thing as of ourselves; but our sufficiency is of God. (2 Corinthians 3:4–5)

God's sufficiency is available. It is not something that you have to go up to heaven to get. You don't have to go to a Bible school or college. You have it right there with you now. God's sufficiency is wrapped up in Christ, and you have Christ.

All that is necessary is that you take advantage of what you have. You may say, "My Father, I am depending upon your sufficiency in Christ to meet this crisis now."

Jesus was made unto us wisdom from God. Wisdom is the most vital thing to each one of us. You may gain vast stores of knowledge, but if you do not have wisdom, you will only waste your knowledge. Just as a foolish man wastes a fortune that his father has made and turned over to him, you can squander the knowledge that you have acquired in riotous living or by throwing it away.

Find out what you are fitted for, then go to it and prepare yourself. Make up your mind that you are going to win. If it is to be a soul-winner, be one of the best the world ever knew. If it is to be a contractor, a carpenter, a mechanic, or a teacher, climb to the top, because Jesus is your ability—your ladder to reach the highest efficiency.

DON GOSSETT

HOW TO GET RID OF
AN INFERIORITY COMPLEX

Many Christians are stifled in their service for the Lord by an inferiority complex. However, you can overcome this through the Word of God. You can be your own faith-builder, for faith comes by hearing the Word of God. (See Romans 10:17.)

You are a new creature in Christ Jesus, which means that the moment you received Christ as your personal Savior and Lord, you were born into God's royal family. You are a son of God. He has created you anew in Christ Jesus. He has put new life into you. You have been born from above, born of the Spirit.

Everything that God creates is good. Therefore, do not run yourself down because your life is in Christ. He made you, and you are what He has made you to be—a new creature. Do not belittle yourself, for you are in Christ, and in Him you have been granted new life. The old life is gone. You are a citizen of a new kingdom. Your citizenship is in heaven.

You are created by God and are His own workmanship. He is now working within you to achieve His own purpose. He is building you up and making you strong in faith. How is He doing this? By His own Word.

Not only are you a new creature in Christ, but you are also made righteous in Him. *"He hath made him to be sin for us, who knew no sin; that we might be made the righteousness of God in him"* (2 Corinthians 5:21). What does it mean to be righteous? It means that you possess the divine ability to stand in God's holy presence without any sense of unworthiness. It means that God has made you righteous with His own righteousness. So now that you are complete in Christ, you can be free from any inferiority complex that once may have held you captive.

You are redeemed from the kingdom of darkness and have been translated into the kingdom of God's dear Son. Once Satan was your lord and master. Then Jesus came into your life and gave you His life. You are now in that great kingdom where He reigns as Lord of Lords and King of Kings. He invites you to join Him and reign with Him in life.

Yes, you are now redeemed, and sin has no dominion over you. In the old kingdom of darkness, you lived under the sway of sickness, fear, poverty, and failure. But now through the blood of Jesus, you have been set free. You can boldly say, "Good-bye sickness, good-bye fear, good-bye lack, good-bye weakness. I am free! Now I live in a new kingdom, the heavenly kingdom, where there is life, light, liberty, joy, peace, health, assurance, blessing, and power. What a redemption is mine. What a Redeemer I have!"

You are an heir of God and a joint heir with Jesus Christ. You have a rich inheritance and are blessed with every spiritual blessing in the heavenly places in Christ Jesus. The Father loves you as He loved the Lord Jesus. He loves you with an everlasting love. You are blessed with heaven's best.

Jesus said, *"I am the vine, ye are the branches"* (John 15:5). That is how closely you are linked with Him. He is the living vine, and you are a branch of that vine. The same life, love, joy, peace, power, wisdom, and ability that flows in the vine flows into the branch. Wherever you go, whatever you do, the vine-life flows through you.

The life of God is in your mortal body right now. It is not just for when you get to heaven; it is for right now. Your spirit has been quickened by the power of God, made alive in Him, and now you live and move and have your being in Christ. (See Acts 17:28.) You have what God says you have. You can do what God says you can do. You are what God says you are.

WHEN THINGS GET HARD

Almost anyone can steer a boat in faith weather, but the storm brings the test. It is when business dies in your hands that it takes courage to face it and find out where the difficulty lays, and with a resolute spirit, correct the abuses and drive the thing on to victory. When your income stops and the money is all gone, what really counts is to face life and conquer. The spirit that wins is the one that remembers it built that business with words and remembers the vibrant thrill that accompanied that creation. He remembers how he could thrill men and make them do what he wanted them to do. Old age cannot rob you of that. All you need is those vibrant, overcoming words.

"But," you say "when I speak those words, there is something inside of me that contradicts them."

Well, go inside of you and drive that something out. That can be done.

You see, there are times when you must go resolutely to the Father, open up your heart to Him, lay the thing before Him, and say, "Now, Father, here is my condition. I want you to so build yourself into me that my life will come to the level of your Word, so that no hard times and no catastrophes can move me, and so that I will face everything as a victor. When everything around me shouts, "Whipped," I will know that I am a victor.

"I will not lose my head nor my heart nor my faith." Drink your cup of gall, but drink it in silence. You are facing life as it is, but you are facing it with God. You are facing it with Omnipotence. Greater is He that is in you than any force that can be against you. (See 1 John 4:4.) You are a conqueror. You are not beaten. The fight is not over yet. You sit down and grow utterly quiet. You remember that God is in you. You remember that you are in Christ, and that all who are in Christ are conquerors. You regard the circumstances around you like the shells and bombs that destroyed Shanghai. But the spirit of Shanghai is not destroyed. She has built a city again. The spirit that is in you is not whipped. You will build the house again. You will build your place in life again. They cannot conquer you. You never think of defeat in connection with your life, for your life is hid with Christ in God where only victory dwells.

DON GOSSETT
DEFEAT THE BLUES

There are various degrees of depression, ranging from a mild case of the "blues" to serious cases requiring psychiatric treatment. Anyone who has ever suffered from depression can testify to its destructive force.

In order to cope with something, you must first recognize its source. Satan is the author of depression. It is one of his favorite tools for ravaging the minds of men and women today.

Evil spirits like depression attempt to oppress you in order to break and crush your spirit. They harass your mind with fear, doubt, and uncertainty. They are the cause of frustration and can destroy your health, your peace of mind, and even the harmony of your home, if you do not take dominion over them.

We have already seen that the Bible commands us to *resist the devil, and he will flee from you* (James 4:7). Refuse to be Satan's dumping ground for mental unsoundness, nervous disorders, or spirits of gloom, heaviness, and depression. Instead, study Matthew 4:1–11 to see how Jesus used the Word of God against the devil. You can do the same thing.

In coping with depression, or anything else that comes from the devil, boldly quote the Word of God against him, just as Jesus did. The Word is a Christian's most effective weapon against the enemy. *"For the weapons of our warfare are not carnal, but mighty through God to the pulling down of strong holds"* (2 Corinthians 10:4).

Know your rights. You are an overcomer. You can defeat all of Satan's works: *"they overcame [Satan] by the blood of the Lamb, and by the word of their testimony"* (Revelation 12:11).

As Christians, we are in a very real warfare with the forces of evil. Read Ephesians 6:10–18 to see what weapons you can use to fight Satan.

Jesus Christ has given you power and authority over all the power of the devil: *"And these signs shall follow them that believe; in my name shall they cast out devils"* (Mark 16:17).

The name of Jesus belongs to you. Dare to use it! Plead the power that's in that name.

Stand your ground fearlessly. Evil spirits of depression know they must submit to that *"name which is above every name: That at the name of Jesus every knee should bow, of things in heaven, and things in earth, and things under the earth"* (Philippians 2:9–10).

Claim the power of God's anointing to disperse Satan's spirit of gloom. *"The yoke shall be destroyed because of the anointing"* (Isaiah 10:27). What is the anointing? It is that supernatural, energizing force within that makes the Spirit-filled life forcible, effective, and productive in Christian service. How do you get it? *"The anointing which ye have received of him abideth in you"* (1 John 2:27). If you're a Christian, it abides in you.

Jesus was the anointed One as He walked on this earth.

> *The Spirit of the Lord is upon me, because he hath anointed me to preach the gospel to the poor; he hath sent me to heal the broken-hearted, to preach deliverance to the captives, and recovering of sight to the blind, to set at liberty them that are bruised, to preach the acceptable year of the Lord.* (Luke 4:18–19)

All of the miracles which Jesus performed while He was here on earth were done through the power of His anointing. *"God anointed Jesus of Nazareth with the Holy Ghost and with power: who went about doing good, and healing all that were oppressed of the devil; for God was with him"* (Acts 10:38).

The anointing is the quality which makes us dynamic for the Lord. It enables us to see Christlike results in our lives. It gives us authority to speak in the name of Jesus against satanic powers—all satanic powers, not just the powers that cause depression.

Psalm 92:10 says, *"I shall be anointed with fresh oil."* The anointing of the Holy Spirit is likened in Scripture to oil. Oil is a type, or "word picture," of the Holy Spirit. On the day of Pentecost, the disciples were all filled with the Holy Ghost. (See Acts 2:4.) Later these same disciples were again filled with the Holy Ghost. (See Acts 4:29–31.) Like the disciples, we too need fresh anointing and infillings of the Holy Spirit.

Jude 1:20 says, *"But ye, beloved, building up yourselves on your most holy faith, praying in the Holy Ghost."* Fervent, anointed prayer in the Holy Ghost builds up our faith.

"But ye have an unction from the Holy One" (1 John 2:20). We should cherish this anointing, this unction that abides within us, and daily yield to the Holy Spirit to impart fresh oil to us.

How do you cope with depression? It is the anointing that breaks the yoke! We can maintain the anointing and overcome depression by a life rich with fellowship with the Lord.

PERSONAL RESPONSIBILITY

To the Christian, responsibility is his response to God's ability. Romans 14:7 reads, *"For none of us liveth to himself, and no man dieth to himself."*

Human society is so constituted that our lives are unconsciously interwoven. The more selfish a man or woman is, the more unhappy he or she is. The more you pour out your life for others, the richer you grow, the fuller your life becomes. Happiness is never attained by gaining, but by giving. *"For God so loved the world, that he gave"* (John 3:16)—He is the first great example of giving. The big life is the giving life; the broader your sympathies, the richer your life becomes. And we are consciously or unconsciously swaying minds about us; the stronger our personality, the more far-reaching our influence is.

The great world forces are spiritual and are expressed in our conduct.

WE ARE BOUND TOGETHER

You can't die without your life touching someone else's. God never intended that our lives be lived alone. His dream was that we should not live alone. His dream was that we should be so entwined in each other that we would all build together. The plan was that we all minister. You do your part, and I do mine; together, we serve and are all fitted together in the body of the Lord.

It is as in the oratorio, the anthem, and the hymn—each one gives its part; or as in the quartette with its soprano, alto, tenor, and bass— together they make a harmonious whole.

PERSONAL WORK

Jesus said to Peter: "I will make you a fisher of men." (See Matthew 4:19.) In that expression, He determines how the gospel shall be propagated. It is going to be by personal contact; it is going to be with single individuals. Jesus' ideal was meeting one or two, as he did with the woman at the well, or Nicodemus. Only a few can do the mass work: Whitfield,

Moody, or Sunday; but the individual work, all can do. Anyone who can talk or write a letter can lead people to Christ. Our responsibility is measured by our ability.

In the early church, there was no advertising department and no newspaper. They were just so thrilled with the message that they just had to give it out to others.

The law that governs personal work is really the love law, found in 1 Corinthians 6:19–20, "*Ye are not your own...ye are bought with a price.*" We are His; He has a right to use us as He pleases. The moment you are born again, you become His redeemed property; and Love, which bought us, has a right to demand our love in return. Furthermore, Jesus has one great mission in the world today: the salvation of men. If we have been bought with a price and belong to Him, then He has a right to direct our activities and determine our life's programs. We are His representatives. All around us are men and women who need Christ; the opportunity of winning men to Christ surrounds us everywhere. And there is nothing that brings such dividends of joy as leading men to Christ. "*The fruit of the righteous is a tree of life; and he that winneth souls is wise*" (Proverbs 11:30). This is the work Christ came to do. He poured His life out that men might be saved; and you must be hands, feet, and heart to represent Him in the world.

Philip said, "*Lord, show us the Father, and it sufficeth us*" (John 14:8). And Jesus said, "*Have I been so long time with you, and yet hast thou not known me, Philip? he that hath seen me hath seen the Father*" (John 14:9). When I saw that for the first time, my heart cried, "Oh, I want to so live that they that have seen me have seen Jesus."

Dr. A. T. Pearson said of George Müller: "George Müller's dream and ambition was to know God and to make Him known."

Let us respond to His ability within us, that He might be made known through us.

DON GOSSETT

THE GIFT OF SLEEP

Are you troubled with insomnia? Do you lie awake and restless some of the night—every night?

In millions of beds, there is a nightly battle. It's the power of God versus the power of Satan. Since God is the author of sleep, a good and necessary gift, then Satan is the author of insomnia. Satan seeks to steal your sleep, thereby destroying your health, peace, and well-being. Sleeplessness breeds nervous disorders, depression, stress, and many kinds of illness.

If you suffer from insomnia, there is a promise in God's Word for you: *"He giveth his beloved sleep"* (Psalm 127:2).

Therefore, you have a sure cure for sleeplessness: you can rout Satan and sleeplessness the way Jesus defeated the devil— by declaring, *"it is written."*

Take your sleep, not by counting sheep, but by quoting God's wonderful Word.

Say, "Devil, IT IS WRITTEN that God gives His beloved sleep, according to Psalm 127:2!"

Say, "Devil, IT IS WRITTEN that I will both lay me down in peace, and sleep: for the Lord makes me dwell in safety according to Psalm 4:8!"

Say, "Devil, IT IS WRITTEN that when I lie down, I shall not be afraid: yea, I shall lie down and my sleep shall be sweet, according to Proverbs 3:24!"

Peace is a prerequisite for sleep. Before lying down at night, through prayer and praise, remove from your mind all anxieties, grudges, resentments, failures, and disappointments.

> *Be careful for nothing; but in every thing by prayer and supplication with thanksgiving let your requests be made known unto God. And the peace of God, which passeth all understanding, shall keep your hearts and minds through Christ Jesus.* (Philippians 4:6–7)

As you cast your cares upon Him, you will find peace. Then you will find it will be easy to go to sleep, free from fear and anxiety in the knowledge that God is watching over you and everything that pertains to you.

E. W. KENYON

BUYING UP YOUR OPPORTUNITIES

No man can get anything worthwhile without sacrifice. We have heard it said, "The world owes me a living." The world owes nothing to anyone. We owe all we are, all we can develop ourselves into; we owe the past a debt we can never pay. We owe the future all that the past has made us and all that the present can develop in us.

Remember that you pay for all that is worthwhile in life. You get nothing that is worthwhile without tears and sweat. Few have success thrust upon them. It comes to most of us through diligent work, intense application, and self-denial. The secret is being able to see opportunities and make them your own.

Mr. Woolworth saw an opportunity in the inexpensive realm of merchandise. Others laughed about it, but he left sixty million dollars behind him. Henry Ford saw that America needed a cheap car. He seized the opportunity and became one of the most outstanding men of his age. All of the great success in the mercantile and mechanical world has been won by men who have had a dream and then translated the dream into dollars and business. There are just as great of opportunities now than as ever. The only difference is that few folks have their eyes open.

I heard a young man say the other day, "What's the use, I'll get an old-age pension when I need it." I believe in old-age pensions, but I know that a great majority of people will drift through life in order to get something for nothing at the end of it.

The secret of success is to be able to open your eyes to see opportunities.

In mechanics, a thousand needs are calling today. In chemistry, the greatest opportunities that were ever offered the human race await us. In the political and educational world, other opportunities are holding their hands out for the coming generation.

Every field awaits pioneers.

DON GOSSETT

AN ATTITUDE OF GRATITUDE

The Bible plainly teaches that God's children are to have a thankful heart, which is an attitude of gratitude. *"Bless the LORD, O my soul, and forget not all his benefits"* (Psalm 103:2). The New Testament commands, *"Be ye thankful"* (Colossians 3:15). The word *thankful* means "to be full of thanks." We should make it a habit of our lives to daily lift our voices in giving thanks to God for His bountiful blessings, as well as express our appreciation to others.

Colossians 2:6–7 declares that when we are truly rooted and built up in Christ and established in the faith, we will be *"abounding...with thanksgiving."* If our lives in Christ are solid and our faith effective, we shall indeed "overflow" with thanksgiving.

The Scriptures warn of the consequence of losing the attitude of gratitude. *"Because that, when they knew God, they glorified him not as God, **neither were thankful**; but became vain in their imaginations, and their foolish heart was darkened"* (Romans 1:21). Ingratitude extinguishes the light of God in the heart. It is the mark of a foolish and hardened heart.

A prominent sign of the last days is the spirit of ingratitude. *"This know also, that in the last days perilous times shall come. For men shall be lovers of their own selves, covetous, boasters, proud, blasphemers, disobedient to parents, unthankful, unholy"* (2 Timothy 3:1–2). Those who are unthankful are fulfilling Bible prophecy.

Luke 17 tells of the ingratitude of nine of the ten lepers whom Jesus healed.

> *And it came to pass, as he went to Jerusalem, that he passed through the midst of Samaria and Galilee. And as he entered into a certain village, there met him ten men that were lepers, which stood afar off: And they lifted up their voices, and said, Jesus, Master, have mercy on us. And when he saw them, he said unto them, Go show yourselves unto the priests. And it came to pass, that, as they went, they were cleansed. And one of them, when he saw that he was healed, turned*

back, and with a loud voice glorified God, and fell down on his face at his feet, giving him thanks: and he was a Samaritan. And Jesus answering said, Were there not ten cleansed? but where are the nine? There are not found that returned to give glory to God, save this stranger. And he said unto him, Arise, go thy way: thy faith hath made thee whole. (Luke 17:11–19)

How often this is the case—ten are healed or blessed in some mighty way, and yet only one turns to God and gives Him the praise and glory due His name. Learn to bless God for the great and mighty things He has done by praising Him daily!

The source of many of our troubles is our tongue. God has prescribed a cure for our "tongue troubles," and that is to use our tongues in praising the Lord. David said, *"I will bless the LORD at all times: his praise shall continually be in my mouth"* (Psalm 34:1). David had learned the secret of victory over his tongue—to keep it busy praising God.

Giving thanks can be more than an expression of gratitude. It can be the victorious fulfillment of the promises of God. Sometimes, they may appear too good to be true. Or could it be that we are not certain that God is sincerely offering something?

God is not a man that He should lie. In Christ, the promises of God are "yea" and "amen." (See 2 Corinthians 1:20.) God is no miser. *"He that spared not his own Son, but delivered him up for us all, how shall he not with him also freely give us all things?"* (Romans 8:32).

Yes, *"all things are yours"* (1 Corinthians 3:21). But it is one thing to hold the title only and yet another to claim possession. To receive a gift is simply to take it from the giver and seal the transaction with the words, "Thank you."

Are you uncertain of your soul's salvation? Then just take God at His Word and say, "Thank You, Lord, for giving me everlasting life through Your Son. I take Your bona fide offer that *'whosoever believeth in him should not perish, but have everlasting life'* (John 3:16)."

Are you burdened by troubles or a lack of peace? Appropriate His all-sufficient grace, which He has promised in 2 Corinthians 12:9, and say, "Thank You, Lord, that Your grace is sufficient for me. I cast my cares upon You. I thank You for the rest You offer those who come to You according to Matthew 11:28, *'Come unto me, all ye that labour and are heavy laden, and I will give you rest.'"*

Does your body need healing? By faith, thank Him for His healing grace and power and say, "Lord, I thank You that *'Jesus Christ* [is] *the same yesterday, and to day, and for ever'* (Hebrews 13:8)." You will be demonstrating your faith by your offering of thanksgiving.

Possess an attitude of gratitude and ever *"be thankful unto him, and bless his name"* (Psalm 100:4).

E. W. KENYON

WHAT ARE YOU WORTH?

What value do you place on yourself, on your time? Your worth in your own eyes is what you will be able to demand in the market. In your heart, you secretly know whether you are true or whether you can be trusted or whether you are worthwhile. If you bluff or pretend, that is what you are. That is your value. Until you, in your own heart, recognize your honesty and worth, you will never come to a level where you can produce wonderful works.

What is your word worth? Have you ever set a price on it? Can those who associate with you and depend on you absolutely trust your word? Really, have you ever set a price upon yourself?

You are too valuable to barter away for a bit of pleasure or frivolous nonsense. You are worth more this year than you have ever been worth before. You are worth more than you think—more to yourself, more to your family, more to the future, more to the firm for which you work.

Allow no month go by without improving yourself. Put self-improvement first. Take an inventory. See what you possess that is worthwhile, what ability you have, what talents you have, and whether they are increasing in value. Find your niche; see where you belong. Find out what you are fitted for and then go to it and win out.

HIGHER LEVEL LIVING

Go on to higher level living in the kingdom of God. Believe you are what God says you are. Think that way. Talk that way. Act that way. Train yourself to live on the level of what is written in God's Word about you.

Do not permit your thoughts, your words, or your actions to contradict what God says about you.

Although you may not master the secret of the positive confession of God's Word in a day, or even a week, you *will* learn it as you continue to walk in it faithfully.

Jesus commanded us to *"have faith in God"* (Mark 11:22)—or to "have the God kind of faith." Then we are told that *"faith cometh by hearing, and hearing by the word of God"* (Romans 10:17). After you hear the Word, then it begins to possess your *heart* and *mouth* as Paul says, *"The word is...even in thy mouth, and in thy heart"* (Romans 10:8).

When a sinner is converted, first, he *believes* on the Lord Jesus Christ and that God raised Him from the dead; then his *confession* is made unto salvation. (See Romans 10:10.)

God fulfills all His promises the same way.

First: You hear the promise—that creates faith.

Second: You believe that promise.

Third: You confess that promise; you talk it; your overflowing heart confesses the Word of promise in gladness and assurance.

Fourth: You act accordingly, and God delights to make it good.

So meditate on the Word of God and all that it has to say for every aspect of your life. As the Word becomes a part of your heart, it will set you free from fear and anxiety and build you up in bold Bible living. Then the abundance of your heart will supply the words of your mouth automatically. Your confession is really a natural overflow of what springs from your innermost being...your heart.

Now, with the truth of God's Word held deep in your heart and springing from your lips, you can freely discover for yourself the wonder of your own bold words!

PERSISTENCE

What we need today in every department of life is a will that cannot be conquered, purpose that overcomes every opposition. We are looking for the one who cannot be conquered, who does not know defeat, and who, regardless of his circumstances, wills to win. We need the one whose will to success governs his life. A man like that is a partner with success, a companion of the overcomer. He couples his imaginations with victory. He lives with the great—the conquerors of all ages. He builds into himself that which makes him win. He eliminates his weaknesses. He dares to face himself and lay his hand upon the thing that hinders progress. He puts himself under a rigid discipline and holds himself steady in the fight.

One can build into one's self the things that ensure success. It requires persistence, stick-to-it-iveness, the "I will not give up" spirit that does not fear self-denial and is not afraid to wear old clothes. The one who is persistent is not ashamed of material or spiritual poverty.

DON GOSSETT

REMEMBER WHO YOU ARE

The story is told that King Richard the Lion-hearted was so successful in defending England that his record was one of continual victory. One time, however, he was outmatched on the battlefield, as combined armies of other European powers were against him.

King Richard the Lion-hearted had a very loyal and trusted servant who always rode by his side in battle and was thrilled by the daring exploits of his king in conquest after conquest.

In this particular battle against the combined armies, the odds were so overwhelming that, for the first time in his brilliant career, King Richard the Lion-hearted sounded a retreat. This was an overwhelming sight for Richard's faithful servant, to see his own brave and noble king leading a retreat.

As the servant ran his horse with King Richard, he remembered battle after battle where the king had so gallantly led the English army to astonishing victory. Now it was a sad, dismal, frustrating defeat.

To conceive of King Richard the Lion-hearted being defeated was more than the trusted servant could endure. So, the story is told, the servant raced his horse right next to the king and shouted in his ear, "King Richard, *remember who you are!*"

These words penetrated the king's heart, and suddenly he gave the command to his bugler to sound a halt to the retreat. Then in a bit of bold strategy, the command was given "to advance and conquer."

According to history, this was the experience that turned back the combined armies that day when King Richard the Lion-hearted suddenly was compelled to remember who he was—a mighty conqueror, a king who had never known or accepted defeat. This is the secret of bold Bible living: *Remember who you are!* Learn to respect what God has placed within you. Read the Bible to learn who you are in Christ.

BE MASTER OF YOURSELF

He who rules himself will be master of circumstances. Self-control fits one for leadership. He who cannot rule his own tongue and temper is an unsafe leader. The first step in the building up of leadership is bringing oneself under strict discipline. If it is necessary that someone else discipline you, and you would break the law if you were not afraid that you would be arrested, you are still unsafe for leadership.

Compel yourself to come into line with your better judgment. Drive yourself to study, to master every subject that you take up. Cultivate habits of thoroughness. Don't allow yourself to be careless. If you are mentally careless, you handicap your future. Be diligent; be on time. You will need no master when you become your own. Rule every faculty. Make them work. Build a strong center self. Out from this center self radiates strength, loyalty to high ideals, and helpfulness. Hold your temper. Control your tongue. Rule your speech. Be master of yourself.

"BE COURTEOUS"

Courtesy has opened more doors than major ability. It does not require an education but an honest heart that loves to serve. That fine old-fashioned courtesy has not all died out. The cream of human kindliness is still sweet and delightful. Plan to give more than is expected of you. Learn beautiful ways of doing common things. Put your best manners on when you awaken in the morning. And wear them through the whole day long. Practice them in your own home so that they will be perfect when you go out into the business world. Little bouquets of lovely words will brighten the room and will open doors for you where you never dreamed. It is as easy to say beautiful things with a kindly spirit as to say mean, unkind things. Put your best self into your words.

Leave the best of yourself lingering in the minds of those who heard you. Courtesy shows heart quality. Your contacts make or break your future. It has opened doors for many that led to success. It will carry you to the top of the hill. No matter how efficient you are, if you lack courtesy and genuine interest in others, you are handicapped.

You can cultivate courtesy as you cultivate English. Be considerate of the aged and the weak. Never laugh at people's eccentricities. Be helpful. It will open hearts and doors for you. Get in the habit of doing this in your own home; then it will be easy when you go outside. Make it a part of your program. Study the fine art of kindliness. Study courtesy as you would study mathematics. Put your finest best into it, and it will pay you dividends through all your life.

DON GOSSETT

OUR IDENTITY IN CHRIST

WHO ARE WE IN CHRIST?

One of my favorite sayings is this: "When you were born again, you were not born to be defeated; you were born to conquer." I believe Romans 8:37, which tells us, *"Nay, in all these things we are more than conquerors through him that loved us."*

We are more than conquerors! We are children of God, dear to Him, and joint heirs with Christ. We have great riches in Jesus! We are heirs of all things. We are who God made us to be. We are a branch of the living Vine, for Jesus said, *"I am the vine, ye are the branches"* (John 15:5). We are the temple of the living God, for the Bible says, *"Ye are the temple of the living God; as God hath said, I will dwell in them, and walk in them; and I will be their God, and they shall be my people"* (2 Corinthians 6:16).

WHAT CAN WE DO IN CHRIST?

We can do all things, whatsoever needs to be accomplished. The Lord gives us the ability to do all He commands of us, so that we can say with Paul, *"I can do all things through Christ which strengtheneth me"* (Philippians 4:13).

WHAT DO WE HAVE IN CHRIST?

We have life; we have light; we have power; we have peace; we have provision for our needs; we have all things that pertain to life and godliness. (See 2 Peter 1:3.) Yes, to be a Christian is more than just being a forgiven sinner. We are heirs of God and joint heirs with Christ Jesus; we are linked with God by the new birth; and we are partakers of His very nature. No wonder we can sing and shout and be glad today, when we know what it really means to be a child of God!

Just remember who you are right in the midst of your battles. Don't accept defeat. Defeat may come and stare you right in the face. Refuse to accept it! Boldly sound a halt to your retreat. Sound the new note of advance and conquer. Yes, you are a conqueror through Christ who indwells your life!

PRAYER POWER

A strange feature about this prayer life is that it reaches to the uttermost parts of the earth. When I pray for a man in London or in Africa, my spirit can send to him through the Father the blessing that he needs today.

The failure of all Christian enterprise is a prayer failure. A church is as powerful as its prayer life. The prayer habit will be born out of your own will. It is most successful when it comes out of self-denial. Prayer is recognition of His lordship, a giving up of much that is not wrong in itself, but hinders and takes our time.

Prayer is facing God with man's needs, with His promise to meet those needs. And prayer alone gives success. Unbelief cannot pray; it can only utter words.

Prayer privilege means prayer responsibility.

Having a prayer life doesn't mean to spend hours in actual prayer but hours of study and meditation in the Word, until the life becomes literally absorbed in the Word and the Word becomes a very part of us. It is simply the voice of faith to the Father.

DON GOSSETT

FINANCIAL SECURITY

Financial security and success is certain when you stand on God's promise to supply all your needs. (See Philippians 4:19.) Let your confession be:

+ No matter how many unpaid bills I have, *my God shall supply all my need.*

+ Regardless of the condition of the economy, *my God shall supply all my need.*

+ Regardless of the size of my bank account, *my God shall supply all my need.*

+ When financial embarrassment stares me in the face, *my God shall supply all my need.*

+ Regardless of the tight money situation, *my God shall supply all my need.*

+ In spite of past financial failures, *my God shall supply all my need.*

+ When things appear all wrong, *my God shall supply all my need.*

+ When things appear all right, *my God shall supply all my need.*

+ Wherever I am, *my God shall supply all my need.*

FAITH FOR FAMILY FINANCES

An open letter to fathers and family providers:

Dear Father:

As a father and the provider for your family, I know how your honest spirit responds to the challenging words of 1 Timothy 5:8, *"But if any provide not for his own, and specially for those of his own house, he hath denied the faith, and is worse than an infidel."*

For the first 11 years, I was the provider for the Don Gossett family, I experienced continual financial hardships and difficulties. Becoming the proud and happy father of five children by the time I was 28 compounded my problems, of course, for there were unrelenting financial requirements. Inability to meet my commitments on time produced embarrassment often. Those unexpected expenditures labeled emergency drained my resources and kept my back up against the wall.

In October, 1961, we were living in the beautiful island city of Victoria, British Columbia. Our financial situation was so deplorable; however, that it was hardly a pleasant experience.

Then, something happened that month that changed our picture in financial matters. What did happen is that after 11 years of defeats and nearly despair, God has ministered to us and through us to meet every need for the last 42 years!

It was an all-night prayer meeting that changed things for us. Joyce and I poured out our hearts to God. Perhaps I shall never forget my wife's prayers that night. I had never heard anyone talk so frankly to our heavenly Father. It wasn't just a nagging, complaining series of utterances either. As we concluded that night of prayer, we were confident that our needs would always be met from that night onward. And they have been, praise God.

God gave me a "secret" of faith for family finances that has never failed. He gave me "My Never Again List," as the foundation for a total change in my life. Point number 2: "Never again will I confess lack, for *'my God shall supply all your need according to his riches in glory by Christ Jesus'* (Philippians 4:19)." The Lord revealed to me how I had limited Him in ministering to my needs, because I constantly talked about my lack of money, my unpaid bills, etc. God asked me from Amos 3:3, *"Can two walk together, except they be agreed?"* I couldn't walk with God in financial supply if I disagreed with Him. How was I disagreeing with God? By disagreeing with His Word. This Word of God became my new testimony. I agreed with God; I disagreed with the devil who was keeping his oppressive hands on the finances. Never again have I been victimized by lack of money for my family.

There are principles I have learned that are God's Word. God honors hard, diligent work. Labor is usually God's way to meet needs. Often God has met my needs by my writings. Writing is hard work. Sitting up all night on a train to deliver a manuscript to a publisher is also tedious. But even more rewarding than the financial returns are the thousands of lives transformed by words I have written under the inspiring leadership of the Holy Spirit.

Not just work, but faith. Your faith is detectible by your words. Second Corinthians 4:13 says, *"We having the same spirit of faith, according as it is written, I believed, and therefore have I spoken; we also believe, and therefore speak."* Faith is released or expressed by your mouth. Speak your faith—that is, speak the Word. Say often, "My God shall supply all my need." Those are seven words that will put you over, even as they have put me over financially. God absolutely watches over His Word to perform it.

There is no doubt about it: What you say is what you get. Speak of your lack of money, of how hard things are going for you, and you will get what you say. I urge you to confess often, "I have faith for finances for my family. Thank you, Father, for thy riches now." With your palms open, reach out to your Father and receive from Him.

PART II:
WORDS THAT BRING TRUST

E. W. KENYON

WITH ALL THY HEART

No man can succeed who is double-minded. No one can win life's fight but he who has a single purpose. Indeed, he who goes into the ring to meet his antagonist must have a single purpose. The Word says, *"Trust in the* LORD *with all thine heart; and lean not unto thine own understanding. In all thy ways acknowledge him, and he shall direct thy paths"* (Proverbs 3:5).

Your work must be with all your heart and subjected to the reasoning faculties. But above all, the lordship of Jesus must absolutely dominate your life.

Paul's words in Romans 1:1 render that he is "the little love slave of Jesus Christ." The great apostle of the Gentiles designates himself as the little love slave of Jesus Christ. Likewise, until your heart is subordinate to the heart of Christ, there will be a division. Reason will try to take the place of revelation.

Second Chronicles 25:2 gives us a picture of a divided heart: *"And he did that which was right in the sight of the* LORD, *but not with a perfect heart."* Here was a king who had every opportunity. He had God right beside Him, if he wanted His company. But yet he had a divided heart, and so he failed.

On the other hand, 2 Chronicles 31:21 is a picture of one who *"did it with all his heart, and prospered."* Here is a man who gave himself over utterly to the will of God, and he prospered.

Do you want prosperity? Go into whatever you do with all your heart. You cannot be a successful preacher with a divided heart. If the husband and wife's hearts have but a single purpose, then the home will be a success. But if there are divided hearts, there will be a divided home.

DON GOSSETT
OVERCOMING FEAR

I have had many interesting discussions with a prominent psychiatrist from Washington, DC, whom I met overseas. We share a concern for the vast numbers of people whose lives are shrouded in fear. Because the giant of fear is slaying its tens of thousands, it is important that Christians embrace God's truth: *"For God hath not given us the spirit of fear; but of power, and of love, and of a sound mind"* (2 Timothy 1:7). As we look to the promises of God's Word, we can possess full assurance that we can live free from fear, for fear has no part in the heart of a redeemed child of God.

There are 365 Scriptures in the Bible that challenge you to live free from fear all the days of your life. So there is a verse against fear for every day of the year!

One such Scripture says, *"Fear thou not; for I am with thee: be not dismayed; for I am thy God: I will strengthen thee; yea, I will help thee; yea, I will uphold thee with the right hand of my righteousness"* (Isaiah 41:10).

Fear need have no part in your heart, for as long as God is with you, you need never fear. He has promised, *"Lo, I am with you alway, even unto the end of the world"* (Matthew 28:20).

God's Word says, *"Fear not: for I have redeemed thee, I have called thee by thy name; thou art mine"* (Isaiah 43:1). Because the Lord has redeemed you, you are delivered from the power of Satan, the author of fear.

"The Lord is on my side; I will not fear: what can man do unto me?" (Psalm 118:6). *"The fear of man bringeth a snare: but whoso putteth his trust in the Lord shall be safe"* (Proverbs 29:25). You need not be snared again by a man-fearing spirit. Because the Lord is with you, man can do nothing to you.

> *"That he would grant unto us, that we being delivered out of the hand of our enemies might serve him without fear, in holiness and righteousness before him, all the days of our life"* (Luke 1:74–75).

"*For he hath said, I will never leave thee, nor forsake thee. So that we may boldly say, The Lord is my helper, and I will not fear what man shall do unto me*" (Hebrews 13:5–6). Because the Lord has said it, you may boldly say the same thing. Because God is your unfailing Helper, you can boldly say, "Fear has no part in my heart!" (See Deuteronomy 31:6; 2 Chronicles 32:7; Psalm 3:6; 27:3.)

Like Joshua, you can stand fearless in the presence of gigantic foes. Like David, you can come against the giants in your life in the all-conquering name of the Lord.

You can be free from fear as God gives you courage, confidence, fearlessness, and the daring to do what His Word declares you can do.

E. W. KENYON

THE LORDSHIP OF LOVE

The LORD *is my shepherd; I shall not want"* (Psalm 23:1). The word
"LORD" here is "Jehovah," and it is a word of three tenses. It represents
the love of three tenses. Psalm 23 is a love song. It is faith's love song. This
particular verse, and the analogy of a sheep and its shepherd, shows the
quiet confidence of long associations. It shows a raptness and simplicity
of faith that is thrilling.

"The LORD is my shepherd" (Psalm 23:1). He is my shepherd indeed.
He is my lover, my caretaker, and my protector. The very word shepherd
suggests protection and care. Is He your shepherd?

"I shall not want" (Psalm 23:1). I shall not want for any good thing. I
shall not want for food; I shall not want for raiment; I shall not want for
shelter; I shall not want for health, for He is the strength of my life.

"He maketh me to lie down" (Psalm 23:2). That is quietness, security,
and rest. If there were enemies, I could not lie down; I would have to stand
on guard, but He is my protection now. My Shepherd Lord shields me
from the enemy.

"He maketh me to lie down in green pastures" (Psalm 23:2). Here is the
causative power of love. The picture is vivid; the clover is up to the knees.
Its luscious beauty charms the eye and satisfies the hungry sheep that
feed.

"He leadeth me beside the still waters" (Psalm 23:2). He leads me beside
gentle waters; clear, rippling waters; the waters of stillness and quietness.
How the heart needs quietness in these troubled days. Every anxiety and
care has been cast upon Him. We are as free as children. By the side of the
stream we rest in security.

"He restoreth my soul" (Psalm 23:3). This is the picture of one who has
become filled with anxiety and fear until he is on the verge of a nervous
breakdown. He restores the troubled, restless, unhappy mind to normal
condition. This is one of the most beautiful facts connected to this divine
care.

When you know that He cares for you and you have every anxiety upon Him, then you will be fresh and happy to do you work. But those burdened with anxiety cannot do much. The Father intended that we would trust Him in utter abandonment. Love is trust and fearlessness.

"He leadeth me in the paths of righteousness for his name's sake" (Psalm 23:3). This is one of the rarest privileges of this wonderful life—to be guided into the realm of righteousness, or into the place where you can stand in the Father's presence, without the sense of inferiority or guilt.

How few have been guided in the paths of righteousness! How few have ever understood the unique, unspeakable privilege of fellowshipping with the Father, of carrying out His will on the earth. You see, when you know this, you can do the work that Jesus left unfinished—healing the sick, feeding the multitude, comforting the brokenhearted—actually walking in His footsteps.

And did you notice this part: *"...for his name's sake."* He leads us for His name's sake. Therefore, shouldn't we take advantage of His name? Shouldn't we use the name of Jesus—that name that has all authority on earth, that name that rules over demons; that name that heals diseases and brings health, strength, and comfort to the heart of man?

Jesus said, *"When he, the Spirit of truth, is come, he will guide you into all truth"* (John 16:13). And the Holy Spirit has come, and He is waiting to guide us into the reality of the unfinished work of Christ, into the reality of righteousness, into the reality of the use of Jesus' name, into the reality of the Father's love and care. Oh, if righteousness were only a reality, even to a few of the members of the body of Christ, we could shake the world!

Hear Him cry, *"Yea, though I walk through the valley of the shadow of death, I will fear no evil: for thou art with me"* (Psalm 23:4). Here is the fearless walk in the realm of spiritual death, surrounded by the forces of darkness, living among those who have only sense knowledge, where demons rule the majority.

This is the sweetest, gladdest walk that's ever known: *"Yea, though I walk through the valley of the shadow of death, I will fear no evil"* (Psalm 23:4). We no longer have to fear disease and sickness, no longer have to fear want and need. Trust in the Lord with utter abandonment, resting upon His Word with a sure, sweet confidence. Simply cry, "I will fear no evil, for you are with me." In His presence, the consciousness of His faithfulness, fear has been destroyed, faith has won the mastery.

Jesus said, *"Lo, I am with you always"* (Matthew 28:20). And how true is this living reality! I know of nothing that can mean more to the believer than to have the consciousness of His presence with them all the time.

"Thy rod and thy staff they comfort me" (Psalm 23:4). The Word and His fellowship are the most priceless gifts to man today. This living Word and the illumination of the Spirit upon it makes life replete.

But hear Him whisper, *"Thou preparest a table before me in the presence of mine enemies"* (Psalm 23:5). This is feasting. You do not eat in the presence of my enemies; you only eat with joy in the presence of friends. Something must have happened to your enemies for you to have a table spread in their presence. The enemies have been conquered. They can no longer injure your heart. The enemies may have been doubt or fear or a hundred other infirmities, but they are conquered.

"Thou anointest my head with oil" (Psalm 23:5). Only two classes are anointed, royalty and the priesthood. You are in the royal family, for your father God is king. You are in the royal priesthood to minister and to show forth the excellencies of Him who called you out of darkness into His marvelous light. The anointing oil of the Spirit is upon you. You are prepared for ministry, the limitless ministry of the God-indwelt, the God-led, and the God-empowered.

"My cup runneth over" (Psalm 23:5). Instead of need and want, you've reached affluence. You have enough for yourself and for others. Your cup is like the widow's cruse of oil. The more you pour out, the more you have. The more you give, the more you possess. The overflowing cup is the cup of blessing.

"Surely goodness and mercy shall follow me all the days of my life" (Psalm 23:6). These are the twins of love—goodness and loving-kindness. These two keep company with you from morning till night. They watch by the bedside.

"And I will dwell in the house of the LORD for ever" (Psalm 23:6). This is the fellowship of the highest order. This is the consummation of redemption. This is the climax of life's dream.

DON GOSSETT
A SOUND MIND

As you overcome the grip of fear, you are then able to think more creatively, more positively. You are able to use your mind to its fullest potential as you are *transformed by the renewing of your mind*" (Romans 12:2). As we have seen in the preceding section, *"God hath not given us the spirit of fear; but of power, and of love, and of a sound mind"* (2 Timothy 1:7).

A sound mind thinks right. Often, you do injustice to the sound mind God has given you by failing to use it. It is not always necessary to seek some mystical direction in spiritual matters. Your sound mind—the gift of God—is quite capable of making sound decisions.

A sound mind avoids negative thoughts. Negative thoughts impede the function of sound thinking and should be avoided.

A sound mind thinks positive thoughts.

A sound mind thinks on the pure, never the impure. This world is contaminated by diseased thinking upon impure and illicit sex.

A sound mind never dwells on this unclean thought pattern.

A sound mind never creates lies or deceit. Since your mind is the source of all words and actions, never permit your mind to entertain untruth.

A sound mind meditates upon the Word of God. Much promise is given in the Scriptures to the value of meditation upon the Word. When you continually meditate upon the Word, you are assured of success and prosperity. (See Joshua 1:8; Psalm 1:3.)

A sound mind is stayed on God. *"Thou wilt keep him in perfect peace, whose mind is stayed on thee"* (Isaiah 26:3).

A sound mind dwells on good reports, not bad. A sound mind remembers the lovely things of life, not the unlovely.

Finally, brethren, whatsoever things are true, whatsoever things are honest, whatsoever things are just, whatsover things are lovely,

> *whatsoever things are of good report; if there be any virtue, and if*
> *there be any praise, think on these things.*   (Philippians 4:8)

A sound mind is a renewed mind, renewed by the Word through the Holy Spirit. A sound mind refuses to harbor grudges, unforgiveness, ill will, and past injustices. A sound mind is a healthy mind, the gift of God.

Affirm these words: "God has given me a sound mind. Through this gift of a sound mind, I can make right decisions and think wholesome thoughts."

E. W. KENYON
GOD UNDERTAKING FOR ME

This is the wonder of the age—that a mere human being can talk to the Creator of the universe, come into actual union with Him, and enter into such relationship with Him that God will become all that he needs. God will become his sponsor, his strength, and his life; He will become his teacher, his comforter, his overcomer, his redeemer, his redemption, and his very life. This is the wonder of the grace of God.

The great Father God actually takes over me as His child; He backs me and makes me see that *"I can do all things through Christ which strengtheneth me"* (Philippians 4:13.) He says to me, *"Fear thou not; for I am with thee: be not dismayed; for I am thy God: I will strengthen thee; yea, I will help thee; yea, I will uphold thee with the right hand of my righteousness"* (Isaiah 41:10).

Think of man, a mere man, coming in contact and union and fellowship with a Being like the creator God. That is what we are doing. That is what Christianity means. Jesus became the link that unites us to the Father. Jesus is the surety of this link. Jesus is the surety of this relationship, this continual fellowship and communion, this continual help and support. He is my surety.

Now, do not give up. Do not let anything happen that will cause you to be discouraged for a moment, because here is the everlasting eternal truth that God is the strength of your life. You need not be afraid of what man can do or what man can say. Trust in the Father with all your heart, and do not lean on what people say nor upon what they think but upon what the Word of God declares. Do not try to work your way through or reason your way through life. Believe your way through. That is the secret of it—believing your way through the problems of life, believing your way over and through the obstacles that confront you daily, just believing that *"greater is he that is in you, than he that is in the world"* (1 John 4:4). It is believing that His wisdom, His strength, and His grace are utterly yours just now.

You will have testing places. You will have times when it seems He has withdrawn Himself from you, but it is only to give you greater joy, greater love, greater power, and sweeter fellowship.

So, fear not; just believe Him!

DON GOSSETT

MAINTAIN PRAISE AND MASTER YOUR FEARS

Living by God's "Pro-Praise—Anti-Fear Principles" produces an abundance of peace, joy, contentmen, and prevailing power!

PRO-PRAISE PRINCIPLES

1. SACRIFICING PRAISE: *"By [Jesus] therefore let us offer the sacrifice of praise to God continually, that is, the fruit of our lips giving thanks to his name"* (Hebrews 13:15).

2. REJOICING PRAISE: *"Rejoice in the Lord alway: and again I say, Rejoice"* (Philippians 4.4).

3. EVERYDAY PRAISE: *"This is the day which the LORD hath made; we will rejoice and be glad in it"* (Psalm 118:24).

4. RESCUING PRAISE: *"When [Jehoshaphat] had consulted with the [Judeans], he appointed singers unto the LORD, and that should praise the beauty of holiness, as they went out before the army, and to say,* **Praise the LORD; for his mercy endureth for ever.** *And when they began to sing and to praise, the LORD set ambushments against the children…which were come against Judah; and they were smitten….and none escaped"* (2 Chronicles 20:21–22, 24).

5. CONTINUAL PRAISE: *"I will bless the LORD at all times: his praise shall continually be in my mouth"* (Psalm 34:1).

6. OMNIPRESENT PRAISE: *"Thou art holy, O thou that inhabitest the praises of Israel"* (Psalm 22:3).

7. ALL-EMBRACING PRAISE: *"Let every thing that hath breath praise the LORD. Praise ye the LORD"* (Psalm 150:6).

Very often throughout each day, I shall whole-heartedly proclaim this God-pleasing phrase of praise: "Praise the Lord!"

ANTI-FEAR PRINCIPLES

1. DEFINING FEAR: *"God hath not given us the spirit of fear; but of power, and of love, and of a sound mind"* (2 Timothy 1:7).

2. OVERCOMING HELPLESSNESS: *"We may boldly say, The Lord is my helper, and I will not fear what man shall do unto me"* (Hebrews 13:6).

3. DEFEATING DEPRESSION: *"Fear thou not; for I am with thee: be not dismayed; for I am thy God: I will strengthen thee; yea, I will help thee; yea, I will uphold thee with the right hand of my righteousness"* (Isaiah 41:10).

4. CONQUERING COWARDICE: *"The fear of man bringeth a snare: but whoso putteth his trust in the LORD shall be safe"* (Proverbs 29:25).

5. SPIRIT OF BONDAGE: *"Ye have not received the spirit of bondage again to fear; but ye have received the Spirit of adoption, whereby we cry, Abba, Father"* (Romans 8:15).

6. TORMENT OF FEAR: *"There is no fear in love; but perfect love casteth out fear: because fear hath torment. He that feareth is not made perfect in love"* (1 John 4:18).

7. DAILY DELIVERANCE FROM FEAR: *"I sought the LORD, and he heard me, and delivered me from all my fears"* (Psalm 34:4).

Very often throughout each day, I shall wholeheartedly proclaim this formula for freedom from fear: "Fear has no part in my heart!"

WORRY DESTROYS EFFICIENCY

Worry is the unhealthy child of *fear* and *unbelief*. These two emotions are married, and what children they have begotten! Worry leads to the wasting of vital energy, the disturbing of digestive and other organs, which impairs your ability. It becomes a mental disease. Almost everyone has it. It is contagious. It leads to all kinds of physical and mental disorders.

But its cure is simple: *"Trust in the LORD with all thine heart; and lean not unto thine own understanding. In all thy ways acknowledge him, and he shall direct thy paths"* (Proverbs 3:5–6). Or, *"[Cast] all your care upon him; for he careth for you"* (1 Peter 5:7). Get quiet for a moment and remember this: God is on your side. If God is for you, who can be against you? (See Romans 8:31.)

Men can't conquer him who trusts in the Lord with all his heart. There aren't enough enemies in all the world to whip the man who trusts absolutely in the wisdom of God, his Father, and does not lean upon "sense knowledge."

No man is safe to go out into the business world until he first has learned the secret of absolute trust in the Lord. So if you haven't learned it yet, and you are bearing your burdens with fretting and care and anxiety, go alone and settle the great issue with Him. Take His wisdom and grace to go out and do your work with perfect efficiency.

There is no salvation in the cross. The salvation is in the Christ who sits on the throne; it is found in the empty tomb. There are many Christians who think I have robbed them of their salvation when I tell them of the truth about the cross. Some churches have no seated Christ, no Savior at God's right hand. They have simply put a dead Christ on the cross. And the people who tell you today that they are living the life of the cross life, clinging to the cross, or trusting in the cross, have no resurrected Christ.

I wonder if you know that it is as bad to sing a lie as to preach it? Think of it: "Jesus, keep me near the cross. There's a precious fountain."

He carried His blood into the Holy of Holies and procured for us an eternal redemption. I don't want to be kept near the cross. Why? Why, we are in Christ. We have the life and the nature of the Father in us.

Jesus said, *"I am the vine, ye are the branches"* (John 15:5). The Vine isn't on the cross. The Vine is in heaven. For it is Christ in you, the hope of glory. (See Colossians 1:27.)

Do you know why some preach the cross and talk about the cross? Because they live in the "sense realm." The cross is something they can see and feel. They can take hold of the little gold cross that is hanging on a chain around their necks or is pinned on the lapel of their coats, and they feel very near something. But Christ is not on that gold cross. Christ is seated at the right hand of the Father. He has put sin away. He has conquered Satan. He has risen from the dead. And, during the forty days, He went and preached to the souls in paradise that had been covered by the sacrificial blood of bulls and goats. He carried them the message of eternal life. He emptied paradise and took them all to heaven. They are there now.

When He carried His blood into heaven and the "supreme court of the universe" accepted it, it was poured out on the mercy seat in the presence of the Father. Then He sat down; and there He is today. His work was finished. His work began on the cross. It ended on the throne. I can't understand why Christians make more of the cross than they do of the seated Christ and of their being seated together with Him.

The cross is where my Lord once hung, where God put our iniquity on Him, where God made Him to be sin for us, where God forsook Him, where God turned Him over to Satan, where sin triumphed, and where God ignored His prayer. No angels ministered to Him there. Darkness cast a veil over Him. The cross is where love went the limit. Christ left His body hanging on the cross. He went to the place where we should have gone and suffered in our stead until every claim was met. Then He was justified in spirit, made alive in spirit. He conquered Satan in spirit as our substitute. Then He entered into His own body, filled with immortality, and He arose from the dead.

DON GOSSETT
SAY GOOD-BYE TO STRESS

Stress is a common denominator among people in all strata of today's society. Everyone is concerned about stress. Best-selling books deal with the subject. Courses are taught about it. Businesses are concerned about the toil it takes on the health and productivity of its employees.

In addition to being a drastically wearing force on our mental and physical functions, stress is actually a killer. It has been discovered to be associated with such maladies as ulcers, heart disease, and even cancer.

Is it possible for the Christian to live free from stress with the world in the shape it's in today? With rapes, muggings, robbery, murder, and disaster threatening us daily? With crises in the economy and the specter of nuclear destruction ever before us?

God's Word has an antidote for stress: *"Thou wilt keep him in perfect peace, whose mind is stayed on thee: because he trusteth in thee"* (Isaiah 26:3).

Instead of worrying that someone in your family will be the victim of rape, robbery, muggings, murder, HIV/AIDS, herpes, heart attack, or cancer, stand in the power of God's Word, which says, *"The angel of the LORD encampeth round about them that fear him, and delivereth them"* (Psalm 34:7). Say, "Devil, *it is written* that no evil shall befall me, neither shall any plague come near my dwelling!" (See Psalm 91:10.)

Instead of worrying about problems on your job, claim the promise of God which says, *"The LORD shall fight for you, and ye shall hold your peace"* (Exodus 14:14). Say, "Devil, *it is written* that the Lord shall deliver me from every evil work!" (See 2 Timothy 4:18.) Say, "Devil, *it is written* that when the enemy shall come in like a flood, the Spirit of the Lord shall lift up a standard against him!" (See Isaiah 59:19.) Remember that God's Spirit is raising a mighty standard of defense in your behalf at the very time others might be putting pressure on you. The battle is not yours, but God's. (See 2 Chronicles 20:15.)

Instead of worrying about how to pay your bills, quote God's promise: *"My God shall supply all your need according to his riches in glory by*

Christ Jesus" (Philippians 4:19). Turn all your cares and worries over to the Lord, for the Word says, *"Cast...all your care upon him; for he careth for you"* (1 Peter 5:7).

The Bible says, *"Commit thy way unto the LORD; trust also in him; and he shall bring it to pass"* (Psalm 37:5). When you fully commit your life to God and place your trust in Him, He will work out every detail of your life.

DON GOSSETT

FULL ASSURANCE OF FAITH

After I received Jesus Christ by faith into my life, there were yet times that I had doubts about my salvation. These doubts were caused by unsaved people who jeered the Bible and things of God. Also, I often pondered if I had the right "feelings" a Christian should have. Then, too, when I would fail the Lord, I wondered if there were anything to my supposedly being saved.

But in my quest, God gave me the *"full assurance of faith"* (Hebrews 10:22) and cured me of all my doubt. Praise His name. How did I attain this full assurance of faith? From God's wonderful Word!

"Nobody can know for sure he is saved." This is what a man told me, whom I once met and shared with him my knowledge of salvation through Christ.

"Never in this life can a person know he is saved," the man continued. "You just must keep on doing the best you can, and when the books are opened, you will find out whether you made it or not."

This worried me. I was trying my best to be a Christian. What if this man is right? As a youngster, this really bothered me.

I cannot say the full understanding of my sure relationship with God came instantly. Rather, it was a matter of learning *"the truth, and the truth shall make you free"* (John 8:32), declared Jesus.

Peace with God. I'm glad I'm a Christian because of the peace with God I gained when I accepted Christ by faith. *"Therefore being justified by faith, we have peace with God through our Lord Jesus Christ"* (Romans 5:1). As long as I resisted the call of the Spirit to accept Christ as my Savior, I was warring against God; I was His enemy, even though He loved me. But then when I ceased resisting and by faith received Him, I had peace with God!

Full Authority to Know. *"As many as received him, to them gave he power to become the sons of God, even to them that believe on his name"* (John 1:12). I received Christ; therefore I knew I was a son of God, His own child. This power I received had changed me, transformed me, made me anew. Hallelujah! O the wonder of receiving Christ, then knowing I was saved.

Another great truth that gave me victory over doubts was this one: *"The Spirit itself beareth witness with our spirit, that we are the children of God"* (Romans 8:16). I received the witness of the Spirit of God, that I belonged to Him. This was precious to know.

Doubts are only cast out by truth. And the truth of God did its work in my heart. *"We know that we have passed from death unto life, because we love the brethren"* (1 John 3:14). When I was saved and knew it, I discovered that hate, grudges, and unforgiveness toward those who had wronged me were gone. I loved others, especially fellow Christians, but God also enabled me to love those who, in the natural order of things, I didn't like. Thank God for His love that passes understanding.

It is not presumption to declare, here and now in this life, that one is saved. *"He that hath the Son hath life"* (1 John 5:12). I knew I had received the Son of God into my heart, and I knew His divine life was within me.

"Therefore if any man be in Christ, he is a new creature: old things are passed away; behold, all things are become new" (2 Corinthians 5:17).

God declares this is His Word. I knew I was a new creature in Christ. This was by His grace, through faith in Jesus Christ.

God had said so, and *"God is not a man, that he should lie"* (Numbers 23:19).

I have deep assurance that one day I will meet Christ face-to-face. My assurance doesn't rest on feelings alone, but on God's Word. And His Word is like an anchor; it holds me steadfast and sure!

WAIT FOR JEHOVAH

More people fail here than perhaps in any other place in the Christian walk. First Samuel 13 is a picture of the great man Saul who failed to wait for Jehovah. I have no heart to condemn him. We have been like Saul. We have failed to wait for the Lord to come to our deliverance. We have taken hold of the thing ourselves.

Wait on the LORD, and keep his way. (Psalm 37:34)

Those that wait upon the LORD, they shall inherit the earth. (Psalm 37:9)

My soul, wait thou only upon God; for my expectation is from him. (Psalm 62:5)

As long as your expectations are from the doctor, from what man can do, the Lord will let you alone, and you can fight it out alone. But, as long as you turn resolutely to Him, He cannot fail you. He will never fail you.

The psalmist wrote, *"I am like a green olive tree in the house of God"* (Psalm 52:8). Why? Because he said, *"I trust in the mercy of God for ever and ever"* (verse 8).

You, too, will be like the green olive tree by the side of the waters stream if you trust Him. But if you do not trust Him, the following verse will describe you: *"He shall be like the heath in the desert, and shall not see when good cometh; but shall inhabit the parched places in the wilderness, in a salt land and not inhabited"* (Jeremiah 17:6).

DON GOSSETT

DO NOT PLAN ON
A NERVOUS BREAKDOWN

It seems almost everyone I meet has just had a nervous breakdown, is in the midst of a nervous breakdown, or else is planning to have a nervous breakdown!" So said the Reverend Jack Hyles, pastor of First Baptist Church, Hammond, Indiana. I agree with Pastor Hyles. Nervous breakdowns have reached almost epidemic proportions in our country today and have become one of the most serious problems currently confronting the medical profession.

One doctor has said that while medical science has conquered many of the deadly diseases which plagued us many years ago, doctors today are facing new illnesses that are just as devastating. Numerous people have fallen victim to these illnesses as a result of the pressures of modern living. They cannot cope with the complexities of our society.

Years ago, I was with an older minister and his wife in a home where we were praying for a woman who had suffered a nervous breakdown. These wise, experienced ministers were speaking to the woman's condition as over and over they affirmed the words of Jesus, *"Peace, be still"* (Mark 4:39). As they kept repeating these life-giving, life-mending words, *"Peace, be still,"* the room was flooded with a peaceful, tranquil atmosphere. The woman responded to the peace of the gospel, and her nervous condition improved immediately.

When during a visit to Israel I had the opportunity of sailing on the Sea of Galilee, I thought how Jesus faced that tempestuous sea long ago. The storm, the fears of His disciples, and the turbulence of those waters were a challenge to Him. Yet He simply spoke, *"Peace, be still,"* and the waters became as calm as a sleeping baby.

Your nervous system may be as troubled as those waters of Galilee were. You may be drowning in inner turmoil. The storms, the pressures, the problems of life may overwhelm you. Yet there is intervention through Jesus Christ our Lord. The words of Jesus are spirit, and they are life. (See John 6:63.) Hear Him speak to you today, *"Peace, be still."*

Just as Jesus had complete dominion over the winds and the waves on the Sea of Galilee, so He has complete dominion over you, your body, and your nervous system. When you speak His words, it is actually the Master of Galilee speaking through you. For did not He say, *"The works that I do shall he do also; and greater works than these shall he do; because I go unto my Father"* (John 14:12)?

Although we are not facing boisterous waves today on an actual sea, we are facing defeat, fearful situations, and sorrow. And at times, like the disciples of Jesus, we are at the point of desperation. But know that Jesus is with you even as He was on that fishing boat in Galilee. He has said, *"I will never leave thee, nor forsake thee"* (Hebrews 13:5); and, *"Lo, I am with you alway, even unto the end of the world"* (Matthew 28:20).

Remember that you are God's child. You were not made for a life of nervous disorder, for frequent bouts with unruly nerves. You were not designed to live a fearful existence. You are God's child, and He loves you. Learn to roll your burdens upon Jesus. Visualize yourself literally placing your problems, your difficulties and care, into His hands. He is a big, loving God, and He has big, kind, capable hands.

Perhaps you have heard it said that no child of God ever needs to have a nervous breakdown or be committed to a mental hospital. This is true—with one condition attached. No child of God who practices a positive praise life will ever have a nervous breakdown or be committed to a mental hospital. For when you joyfully praise God, you are dispelling the negative forces that produce nervous breakdowns.

A dear Christian who had suffered from a nervous problem wrote to me recently saying, "For more than three years I have been plagued by a severe nervous problem. I have hesitated to say it was a complete nervous breakdown, for I have proudly tried to avoid that term. Perhaps it has been a nervous breakdown. At least, it has been a tormenting time for me and for my dear family.

"I was encouraged by some friends to tune in to your program. I can hardly express in words the help I have received through your ministry. Mainly, your emphasis on praise-power has helped me immensely."

Most nervous problems are caused by the "CDTs." What are the CDTs? you might ask. Some new modern disease? No, it is not exactly a modern condition, although it has grown in prominence in recent times. The CDTs simply stand for "Cares, Difficulties, and Troubles." It is learning to cope with the CDTs of life that brings to many a real challenge of faith.

Here is how you can overcome a nervous disorder by practicing God's order:

1. *"Cast...all your care upon him; for he careth for you"* (1 Peter 5:7). Do you have a lot of problems, cares, and difficulties today? Don't carry them in your own mind, on your own shoulders. Cast them upon the Lord. Let go of them and let God have them. And leave them with Him. Picture your nervous disorder as like the tempestuous Sea of Galilee with its boisterous, rolling waves. Arise in the name of your Savior and speak to those nerves as Jesus did to that sea: *"Peace, be still"* (Mark 4:39). There is amazing power in those words. They are the words of the mighty Creator Himself speaking to His creation. So speak them today.

2. Praise the Lord. Praise elevates your soul to that lofty realm, where the Spirit of God is soaring. Praise is in harmony with God's complete expectation of your good life. Discipline your lips to praise the Lord. *"By him therefore let us offer the sacrifice of praise to God continually, that is, the fruit of our lips giving thanks to his name"* (Hebrews 13:15).

So many people who have nervous trouble are prone to complaining, to seeking justification for their condition. You must stop such negative, gloomy talk, or you will never be set free. That is why I stress: Discipline your lips to praise the Lord.

This is God's remedy for a nervous breakdown. Try God's way and experience for yourself His deliverance.

FEAR HAS NO PART IN MY HEART

Fear has one source: the devil. *"For God hath not given us the spirit of fear; but of power, and of love, and of a sound mind"* (2 Timothy 1:7). I want you to notice that according to the Word of God, fear is not a mental quirk. It is not an imagination or a feeling, but an actual spirit that is given to us, not by God, but by Satan.

The results of fear are not pleasant. In fact, the Bible says that *"fear hath torment"* (1 John 4:18). Victims of fear often suffer physical agony, mental anguish, and spiritual torment.

Furthermore, fear is deceptive. Because of fear, people will rush into traps that are laid for them by the devil. *"The fear of man bringeth a snare"* (Proverbs 29:25). Fear leads astray, beguiles, and deludes.

Fear produces in-kind, just as faith produces in-kind. If you believe God will heal you—He will! If you fear the devil will afflict you with cancer—He will! Thus, the fear of disease can actually produce disease; the fear of calamity can actually bring that calamity upon you; fear failure, and you open the door for failure to engulf your life. This is what happened to Job: *"For the thing which I greatly feared is come upon me, and that which I was afraid of is come unto me"* (Job 3:25). Defeat, depression, disease, destruction, and even death were the result of Job's fears.

Fear is destructive, leading some even to the brink of suicide. Fear causes sleeplessness, nervous breakdowns, oppression in your prayer life, and bondage in witnessing. Fear causes you to expect the worst. It grips you like a vise.

Dare to rebuke fear in the name of Jesus. Call the author of fear by his right name: Deceiver, Liar, Fraud. *"Resist the devil, and he will flee from you"* (James 4:7).

Stephanie Adams of Sydney, British Columbia, who had been a victim of fear, wrote to me:

> Before I heard your radio broadcast, fear used to grip me like a vise no matter where I went. I prayed always for God's help, and

I know He answered by leading me to listen to your broadcast. Now I've learned how to cast out all fear in the name of Jesus. I'm trusting God completely now, and I am a positive Christian. I thank the Lord for using you in this way.

Mr Robert Clark of Moose Jaw, Saskatchewan, wrote:

Your messages on fear are helpful and interesting. So many people have phobias and superstitions about this and that, as you describe, and they make life difficult for themselves and others. So your message on this subject must do an immense amount of good to those who are in bondage to such beliefs. I trust that many will be persuaded to turn their problems over to God and find deliverance.

Because God is with you, you need no longer fear. *"Fear thou not; for I am with thee: be not dismayed; for I am thy God: I will strengthen thee; yea, I will help thee; yea, I will uphold thee with the right hand of my righteousness"* (Isaiah 41:10).

THE CREATIVE POWER OF BELIEVING

We know that believing is having. It is possession. God believed the universe into being. He whispered, *"Let there be,"* and it became. And God has given us the ability to believe things into being when He said to us, *"All things are possible to him that believeth"* (Mark 9:23). He was laying down the law of faith. It is not only the law, but it is an invitation to go into the realm where that law reigns.

Jesus believed in His own words. When He said, *"Lazarus, come forth"* (John 11:43), He knew that Lazarus would come. When He said to the demon, *"Come out of him"* (Mark 9:25), He knew the demon would come out. When He said to the sea in the midst of the storm, *"Peace be still"* (Mark 4:39), He knew that the sea would obey. Jesus believed. When He told Peter to catch a fish and open its mouth and take out money to pay their poll tax, He knew that the money would be there. (See Matthew 17:27.) He believed maimed legs whole. He believed the lepers clean. He believed that the bread would multiply until it fed five thousand. He believed that the water would sustain His weight when He walked on the sea. He believed the water into wine.

He is challenging you to believe in your word, or in His Word on your lips.

DON GOSSETT

UNTROUBLED HEARTS

If your heart is filled with fear, you will talk fear, and your fears will increase. The amazing thing is that when you speak, those fears immediately grip you tighter than ever.

To overcome this, fill your heart with the Word of God. Then, when you are tempted to doubt, make your lips speak His Word instead of your doubts. Simply make a decision to have your lips voice the Word instead of fear. You can do it through the Lord Jesus Christ who will give you the strength. (See Philippians 4:13.)

Because He hath said, *"Fe Fear thou not; for I am with thee: be not dismayed; for I am thy God"* (Isaiah 41:10), we may boldly say, "I am no longer afraid because God is with me all the time."

Because He hath said, *"God hath not given us the spirit of fear; but of power, and of love, and of a sound mind"* (2 Timothy 1:7), we may boldly say, "I am free from all fear because my God hath not given me fear, but power, love, and a sound mind."

Because He hath said, *"My peace I give unto you....Let not your heart be troubled"* (John 14:27), we may boldly say, "'Being justified by faith, we have peace with God through our Lord Jesus Christ' (Romans 5:1), 'for he is our peace' (Ephesians 2:14), and therefore my heart is not troubled or fearful."

Because He hath said, *"Thou wilt keep him in perfect peace, whose mind is stayed on thee: because he trusteth in thee"* (Isaiah 26:3), we may boldly say, "I have His perfect peace because my mind is stayed on Him."

DON GOSSETT

HALLELUJAH LIVING

In my travels as a missionary evangelist, I have ministered to people who speak many different languages. God has ordained that there is only one universal word, virtually the same in every language. It is the word *hallelujah*. Next to the name of Jesus, it is the most powerful word spoken by Christian lips.

The word appears many times in the Jewish Scriptures, where it is simply "hallelujah." In the King James Version, it is translated, *"Praise ye the LORD."*

Hallelujah is more than a word; it is a song of praise. How often I have seen the lowliest sinner saved by grace overwhelmed by the thankfulness in his heart—his new language is "Hallelujah!" Does the highest archangel desire to magnify the name of the One who sits on the throne of heaven? An hallelujah bursts from his lips, resounding through the corridors of the skies. Hallelujah is the common language of redeemed sinners, saints, and angels.

If you are young, praise the Lord for the prospect of health and for the length of days in which to serve Him. If you are older, praise God for the blessings of your years and for the many benefits you have received.

"Praise ye the LORD [hallelujah]. *O give thanks unto the LORD; for he is good: for his mercy endureth for ever"* (Psalm 106:1). Hallelujah expresses thanksgiving, praise, and worship.

All who have found that the Lord is gracious and full of compassion should have a song of praise in their hearts. Hallelujah is a natural and joyous chorus of praise welling up in the redeemed heart to magnify God. *"It is a good thing to give thanks unto the LORD, and to sing praises unto thy name, O most High"* (Psalm 92:1).

Hallelujahs fill heaven. It is a word that will be prominent in our vocabulary there. *"I heard a great voice of much people in heaven, saying, Alleluia"* (Revelation 19:1).

Hallelujah-living is based on the cardinal truth of Romans 8:28: *"And we know that all things work together for good to them that love God, to them who are the called according to his purpose."* It is boldly proclaiming hallelujah in the face of difficulties, troubles and problems, emphatically believing that *"all things"* are working together for our good and God's glory.

The wife of a pioneer preacher in Oregon said hallelujah each time she passed her often-empty refrigerator. God filled it and kept it filled as she practiced hallelujah-living.

A Christian saleswoman, working on commission in a prestigious department store in Seattle, heard the story of the empty refrigerator. Inspired, this lady began saying a quiet hallelujah for increased sales at work each time she passed the cash register. Her sales took off, and she thanked God, along with her hallelujahs, on each trip by the cash register.

An unemployed carpenter in Regina, Saskatchewan, immediately got a job when he began to practice hallelujah-living. A man in Tulsa, Oklahoma, laid off at a large plant, took the faith position of hallelujah-living, and, by a miracle, a job was opened to him.

Hallelujah-living is obeying 1 Thessalonians 5:18: *"In every thing give thanks: for this is the will of God in Christ Jesus concerning you."* It is shouting hallelujah in the face of every circumstance of life, good or bad.

Hallelujah-living is following the examples of those in the Bible who, by praising God, triumphed in the face of certain defeat. Consider Jonah swallowed by the whale, the Israelites marching around Jericho, Judah surrounded by three armies, and Paul and Silas imprisoned in the Philippian jail.

Is there any magic in the word *hallelujah*? No. Directed toward God in childlike faith, it simply means "Praise ye the Lord." It is taking the bold faith attitude that God is in all, above all, and inhabits the praises of His people. (See Psalm 22:3.)

E. W. KENYON
"ASK, AND IT SHALL BE GIVEN YOU"

"Ask, and it shall be given you; seek, and ye shall find; knock,
and it shall be opened unto you."
—Matthew 7:7

Ask, and it shall be given you" has a ring of finality, and also of reality. It is the voice of God on the lips of the Master, Jesus. What He says, is. Jesus said, "It shall be," and what He said shall be, is.

As your heart grows accustomed to the reality of the Word, faith becomes an unconscious working force in you. You do not have to think about making your fingers act as you wish to pick up a book. Your hand instinctively reaches forth, grasps it, and brings it to you. Likewise, you do not have to think of faith. Faith functions unconsciously.

Jesus was never faith-conscious any more than He was righteousness-conscious. He was the author and finisher of faith even when He walked the shores of Galilee.

We are the children of faith. We should never be conscious of it, never think of it, never feel the need of it. A child does not feel the need to have faith in his father or mother. A great calamity must take place before that, and when a child does not feel the need of faith in his parents, something unspeakable has happened that has utterly "unfaithed" him and destroyed the thing that God and nature planted in him.

By the new birth, you come into the family. It is no longer a faith problem then; it is merely a problem of getting acquainted with the Father and living in fellowship with the Master, until this faith becomes unconscious fact that grows out of this conscious fellowship.

The trouble is that we have made a religion out of the relationship, and our redemption is a theoretical thing instead of reality. But Jesus said "It shall be," and so then it is. We may rest quietly on His Word.

DON GOSSETT

COLD FEET AND A YELLOW STREAK

"The fear of man bringeth a snare."
—Proverbs 29:25

Cold feet and a yellow streak is fear and a lack of courage, bordering on cowardice. What are the symptoms? You would be used of God, but you are afraid of people's opinions of you. You would speak up for Jesus, but you are hemmed in by the fear of man. You would be bold in using the name of Jesus, but you withhold because you are afraid of failure, or that someone may criticize you. You would love to place your hands upon the sick for recovery, but you draw back because you are afraid you would be branded a "healer" or a fanatic. God warns, *"Now the just shall live by faith: but if any man draw back, my soul shall have no pleasure in him"* (Hebrews 10:38).

As a child, I had a bad case of cold feet and a yellow streak. The first day I entered school, I kept my head on my desk all day long, because I didn't want to look at others, or have others look at me. When visitors would come to our home, I would hide away in a closet or crawl under a bed, so I wouldn't have to meet strangers. What hang-ups! But how real they were! I have had a lifelong battle with a tendency to avoid eye contact with people, likely another symptom of this ailment cold feet and a yellow streak. When I was elected president of my high school student body, I fumbled with words as I led those student body assemblies that were agony to me. Also, I have had to wrestle with an overly sensitive man-pleasing attitude.

But God has helped me. I am debtor to help you that are captives to cold feet and a yellow streak. I took the words God spoke to Moses. *"Now therefore go, and I will be with thy mouth, and teach thee what thou shalt say"* (Exodus 4:12). God promised to be with my mouth, even as He was with Moses' mouth. I learned to speak freely, instead of faltering, hesitant speech.

Here are key prayers I've employed in overcoming cold feet and a yellow streak. Daily I make my earnest prayer, the same prayer God so mightily answered for the early Christians: *"And now, Lord, behold their threatenings: and grant unto thy servants, that with all boldness they may speak thy word, by stretching forth thine hand to heal; and that signs and wonders may be done by the name of thy holy child Jesus"* (Acts 4:29–30). Another strong prayer: *"[Grant] that utterance may be given unto me, that I may open my mouth boldly...that therein I may speak boldly, as I ought to speak"* (Ephesians 6:19–20). This has given me authority in God-given bold speech. What a contrast when governed by cold feet and a yellow streak and its characteristic negative, reluctant speech habits!

I challenge you: Be done with cold feet and a yellow streak (fear and cowardice). Life is too short to be fettered by a fear of man's opinions. When God desires to flow through you in one of the gifts of the Holy Spirit or be used of Him in supernatural ministry to the oppressed, fearlessly step out to be used of Him.

When I have faced crowds of tens of thousands night after night in India in our crusades, how grateful I was that God had delivered me from cold feet and a yellow streak. The bolder my faith, the greater the victories in salvation of multitudes and the healing of the sick.

I charge you: Be done with cold feet and yellow streak. God has not given you the spirit of fear, but of power, and of love, and of a sound mind. (See 2 Timothy 1:7.) There's a verse against fear for every day of the year. Fortify yourself from these words: *"For he hath said, I will never leave thee, nor forsake thee. So that we may boldly say, The Lord is my helper, and I will not fear what man shall do unto me"* (Hebrews 13:5–6). Love the brotherhood. Honor all men. But never fear any man, nor what man can do unto you.

What you confess is what you possess. What you is what you get. Say it boldly. "God sets me free from every spirit of fear. I am no longer bound by man's opinions. I am free in Jesus. I will daringly do God's will for my life. I shall be bold in being used of God. With all confidence I shall minister in Jesus' name, no man forbidding me. Fear has no part in my heart!"

PART III:
WORDS THAT BRING HEALING

DON GOSSETT

THE ALPHABET OF BOLD LIVING

The following is what I call my "Alphabet of Bold Living." It covers many Scriptures that are our footholds for bold Bible living. Learn them and allow them to become a part of your heart. Then move out in bold exploits for God!

A: *"All boldness to speak thy Word"* (Acts 4:29).

B: *"Bold in our God"* (1 Thessalonians 2:2).

C: *"Come boldly unto the throne of grace"* (Hebrews 4:16).

D: *"Draw nigh to God, and he will draw nigh to you"* (James 4:8).

E: *"Endued with power from on high"* (Luke 24:49).

F: *"Filled with the Holy Ghost, they spake the word of God with boldness"* (Acts 4:31).

G: *"Great is my boldness of speech"* (2 Corinthians 7:4).

H: *"Having boldness to enter into the holiest by the blood of Jesus"* (Hebrews 10:19).

I: *"I can do all things through Christ which strengtheneth me"* (Philippians 4:13).

J: *"Joy of the LORD is your strength"* (Nehemiah 8:10).

K: *"Know the truth, and the truth shall make you free"* (John 8:32).

L: *"Lo, he speaketh boldly"* (John 7:26).

M: *"Much bold in Christ"* (Philemon 8).

N: *"Nothing ashamed, but with all boldness, as always, so now also Christ shall be magnified in my body, whether it be by life, or by death"* (Philippians 1:20).

O: *"Obey God rather than men"* (Acts 5:29).

P: *"Paul spake boldly in the name of the Lord Jesus"* (Acts 9:29).

Q: *"Quench not the Spirit"* (1 Thessalonians 5:19).

R: *"Righteous are bold as a lion"* (Proverbs 28:1).

S: *"Saw the boldness of Peter and John...they took knowledge of them, that they had been with Jesus"* (Acts 4:13).

T: *"That we may have boldness in the day of judgment"* (1 John 4:17).

U: *"Utterance may be given unto me, that I may open my mouth boldly, to make known the mystery of the gospel...that I might speak boldly, as I ought to speak"* (Ephesians 6:19–20).

V: *"Very bold"* (Romans 10:20).

W: *"We may boldly say"* (Hebrews 13:6).

X: *"Wax bold"* (Acts 13:46).

Y: *"Ye are not your own...ye are bought with a price"* (1 Corinthians 6:19–20).

Z: *"Zealous of good works"* (Titus 2:14).

E. W. KENYON

DIVINE COOPERATION

"It is God which worketh in you."
—Philippians 2:13

The sense of mental weariness is common with all brain workers. It is common with all those who are bearing burdens, whether it be a mother, or a stenographer, a mechanic, or the head of a big enterprise.

The sense of mental weariness is that period when the brain almost ceases to function. In these days of high pressure, these periods occur too frequently.

Is there any way for us to come in contact with a refreshing stream of inspiration and life, health and strength? Yes! And we believe we have found it. Since Christ came in to make our bodies His home, there has come with increasing frequency the consciousness of His enabling, of His working and abiding strength.

When we learn the secret of depending upon Him who has come to abide within us, we will discover the spring of eternal mental and spiritual youth. That spring of eternal youth is the *"God which worketh in you."*

No matter how tired you are, you can hook up with Him. You can switch off, and He can switch on. He will take your place and think thoughts in and through you. His vibrant energy and clear mind can take the place of your tired, jaded mind. There is within you this living, vital force that claims a right to think through your faculties and to further reveal Itself through your faculties. Christ desires to unveil the very dreams and purposes of God in you.

When you feel the sense of limitation, rest in Him. Call Him upon the scene. Learn, in everything that you are doing, to put the burden upon Him. Learn to trust His energy for the thinking, for the planning, for the physical strength.

His greater wisdom and ability is there. His patience, His steadfastness, His wisdom, and His unconquered courage is there. He can make real in your life His dream of the ages. Learn to depend upon Him.

You ask how? The next mental effort, the next burden, the next decision you have to make, call on Him. Call on Him in this sense and be confident that He is in you and He is willing to cooperate with you.

Call upon Him. Let Him know you are resting upon Him for courage, strength, wisdom, and quietness. Just say, "I am expecting that if I have lost my courage and grit, it will be Your opportunity to show Your strength and ability in me."

Rest in His rest; be so strengthened in His strength and so upheld in His upholding power that you face life with joy. Face your problems with the consciousness of victory. You know that you cannot fail, for the unfailing One is your all in all. Underneath are the everlasting arms and behind are the infinite resources of God. He won't allow you to fail, and with joy you can face every problem. You look at circumstances and laugh at them. You look at the environment and smile as you see it melt in the presence of Omnipotence.

"Blessed is the man that trusteth in the Lord, and whose hope the Lord *is."*   (Jeremiah 17:7)

DON GOSSETT

PLEASANT WORDS ARE HEALTH TO THE BONES

"Pleasant words are as an honeycomb,
sweet to the soul, and health to the bones."
—Proverbs 16:24

Pleasant words are pleasing to God. Words pleasing to God are in harmony with His own Words, and they are what He directs us to speak.

God declares, *"Whoso offereth praise glorifieth me"* (Psalm 50:23). Pleasant words—words pleasing to God—are words of praise and words spoken in harmony with the Word. These pleasant words of praise produce health benefits. When praise becomes a way of life, God is glorified and manifests the benefits of His salvation. Salvation includes healing!

Satan the oppressor (see Acts 10:38) is the cause of our health problems and mental disturbances. But Satan is allergic to praise; so where there is massive, triumphant praise, Satan is paralyzed, bound, and banished. Praise produces the atmosphere where God's presence resides. (See Psalm 22:3.) Therefore, praise is the most effective shield against Satan and his attack. Praise is the signal to Satan of his defeat; it's the most devastating weapon we can use in our conflict with Him.

When David Wilkerson was in the early part of his work among the gangs of New York City, he encountered a group of boys on a street corner. As he approached them, there were signs that they were preparing to attack. Looking to the Lord for guidance, David continued to advance. At the instant they seemed poised to strike, David suddenly clapped his hands and shouted, "Praise the Lord." The entire gang broke ranks and fled. The only plausible explanation for the action is that these boys were activated by evil spirits who panicked at the shout of praise. Pleasant words of praise spoken by David proved to be literal health to his bones!

"Pleasant words are as an honeycomb, sweet to the soul, and health to the bones" (Proverbs 16:24). The reverse of this Scripture would read:

"Unpleasant words are bitterness, unforgiveness, malice, devastating to the soul, and will destroy your health and well-being."

Pleasant words are not just nice little dainties. Pleasant words are powerful, because they harmonize with heaven, administer health benefits, and are characterized by much praise!

DON GOSSETT

THE LORD IS THE STRENGTH OF MY LIFE

The Lord is the strength of my mind; so today I think sound, healthy thoughts. I think upon those things that are true, honest, just, pure, lovely, and of a good report. (See Philippians 4:8.) A strong mind is a positive mind, the mind of Christ. And "[I] *have the mind of Christ*" (1 Corinthians 2:16).

The Lord is the strength of my ears, so I hear well today. Seven times in Revelation 2 and 3 the command comes, "*He that hath an ear, let him hear what the Spirit saith.*" Most important, with my renewed, sound, strong mind, I hear what the Spirit says unto me.

The Lord is the strength of my eyes, so I have good vision for today. I see others through eyes of love, kindness, and goodwill.

The Lord is the strength of my mouth, so I speak those words that are edifying, ministering grace to those who hear me. Isaiah 50:4, "*The Lord God hath given me the tongue of the learned, that I should know how to speak a word in season to him that is weary: he wakeneth morning by morning, he wakeneth mine ear to hear as the learned.*" I refrain from speaking those words that are negative, destructive, corrupt, critical, harsh, or unkind.

The Lord is the strength of my heart, so I have a good sound heartbeat for today. My prayer is, "Lord, be thou the strength of my physical heart, as long as I serve you on this earth. Yea, seventy years and by reason of strength eighty years or more." Oh heart, do your good work for this day.

The Lord is the strength of my hands, so that whatsoever my hands find to do, they do it with all their might.

The Lord is the strength of every organ, tissue, bone, fiber, nerve, and cell in my body. The Lord is the strength of my life from the top of my head to the soles of my feet.

The Lord is the strength of my life—my whole life—spirit, soul, and body. He infuses strength into the hidden man of the heart.

My affirmations for today:

The people that do know their God shall be strong, and do exploits.

(Daniel 11:32)

The LORD will give strength unto his people; the LORD will bless his people with peace. (Psalm 29:11)

I can do all things through Christ which strengtheneth me [not weakeneth me]. (Philippians 4:13)

The joy of the LORD is [my] *strength.* (Nehemiah 8:10)

As [my] *days, so shall* [my] *strength be.* (Deuteronomy 33:25)

When I am weak, then am I strong. (2 Corinthians 12:10)

I affirm it five times:

"The Lord is the strength of my life."
"The Lord is the strength of my life."
"The Lord is the strength of my life."
"The Lord is the strength of my life."
"The Lord is the strength of my life."

I think strength. I believe in the Lord's strength. I talk strength. Joel 3:10 says, *"Let the weak say, I am strong."* I confess that I am strong. Often I say, "Strength, strength, strength," as I speak the Word to my Spirit. Praise the Lord.

IMAGINE THIS SCENE IN HEAVEN

I can imagine the Father asking, "Why is that woman crying down there?"

One of the angels answers, "She is trying to get her healing."

Then the Father turns to Jesus and says, "Haven't you born her diseases?"

Jesus answers, "Yes, I bore them."

"Then what is the matter?"

An angel speaks up and says, "She just doesn't know that she is healed."

It is when you take your place as a son or a daughter of God and take what belongs to you that you arrive. You don't have to be sick. You don't have to stay in poverty and want. If you stay there, it's because you've educated yourself to stay there. Philippians 4:19 says, "My God shall supply all your need."

You say, "That is true," and go right on living in poverty. You talk about your weakness and lack of strength. You talk about your sickness.

His Word cannot fail you if you act upon it and talk about it. No word from God is void of power. You must say, "What the Bible says is true," and then act as though it were, instead of repudiating it by your actions. If you have pain anywhere, you may say in your distress, "Father, what does this mean?" But you should absolutely refuse to have it. You must boldly rebuke it in the name of Jesus Christ, and it must leave.

Until the Word becomes a living thing to us, we will always be looking for our healing. It does not mean that we must try to believe the Word. You don't try to believe the truth. It is like a woman whose husband is a drunkard. She tries to believe in her husband, although she knows he lies to her. Is God like that? It is blasphemous to talk like that. A boy might just as well say about his father who has never lied to him, "I am trying to believe in my father."

This is the living Word that cannot fail. No Word of God can fail. You don't need to try to believe in His Word.

John 15:7 says, *"If ye abide in me, and my words abide in you, ye shall ask what ye will, and it shall be done unto you."*

You make that Scripture your own. You don't need any other Scripture.

Also, you can whip the devil with this one: *"Hitherto have ye asked nothing in my name: ask, and ye shall receive, that your joy may be full"* (John 16:24). This applies to finances, debts, sickness—*everything.*

Let us begin to act as though this Word were true. His Word cannot fail the man who acts upon it.

DON GOSSETT
GLADNESS: A SECRET TO STRENGTH

Greater than any human pleasure or happiness is the joy of the Lord. Joyful Christians are the best advertisement for Christianity. Joyful Christians have always been a challenge and testimonial to a broken-hearted world.

Happiness is the product of our surroundings. It is the thing that satisfies the senses. The material things that bring one happiness may be taken from him in a moment, and he is left desolate.

Joy belongs to the spiritual realm just as happiness belongs to the sense realm. When a Christian is not joyful, it is either because of broken fellowship or a lack of knowledge of what he is in Christ. It is this unspeakable joy which makes you triumphant over the petty trials of life, and a victor over the testings that may come.

John said the purpose of our fellowship life was that we might have fullness of joy. (See 1 John 1:3–4.) Joy cannot be full without full fellowship. It is this joy of Christianity that makes Christianity the most attractive thing in the world. When joy goes, the Word loses its power, its freshness, and its richness. It is only when fellowship is at flood tide and your heart is filled with joy that God is honored and souls are saved.

Fellowship, in its fullness, is the joy life with the throttle wide open on a downgrade. Yes, this joy of the Lord is one of the greatest things that comes to us in the new birth. It makes trouble lose its grip upon us; makes poverty lose its terror. Remember that Jesus said, *"If ye keep my commandments, ye shall abide in my love; even as I have kept my Father's commandments, and abide in his love. These things have I spoken unto you, that my joy might remain in you, and that your joy might be full"* (John 15:10–11).

Again, we consider the difference between joy and happiness. Both are to be desired; but it is far more important that we have joy than mere earthly happiness. Happiness depends on the things that we have or own, like property or loved ones. But joy is a thing of the spirit. It is an artesian well in the spirit that bubbles up and overflows. It is the thing that comes as a result of the Spirit's working in our lives.

We read that the martyrs had joy unspeakable even when dying in physical agony. It stirred the multitudes that thronged about and startled men: How could they be so full of joy when they knew that death was near?

I've witnessed many Christians going through deep sorrow who have been kept by this unquenchable joy.

In years of evangelism, I've observed that joy is the real secret of evangelism. In our meetings, I've noticed that it is the joyful, living testimony that stirs the people. It is the person who is so full of joy that he can hardly speak, as the tears stream down his face, that moves the people. Yes, it is indeed the joyful testimony that touches hearts.

When we speak the Word with assurance and joy, it brings conviction to the listeners. When the Word becomes more real to you than any word man has ever spoken, your lips will be filled with laughter, your heart will be filled with joy, and you will have a victorious Christian life.

How many times I have seen that the hesitant testimony is a forerunner of failure, and the joyful testimony is a forerunner of victory. Christians are only as strong as they are filled with joy of the Lord. A church is only as strong and influential for Christ in a community as it is filled with real joy of the Lord. Why? *"The joy of the LORD is your strength"* (Nehemiah 8:10). When people complain of lacking strength, or talk about how weak they are, often their real lack is the joy of the Lord.

When the Israelites returned from Babylon to rebuild the walls of Jerusalem, Nehemiah found many of them were mourning and weeping, some were suffering with diseases, and others were weak and undernourished. Not a few were downcast, defeated, and despondent. But Nehemiah asked God for help for his people, and God gave them the message through their leader: *"This day is holy unto the LORD your God; mourn not, nor weep. For all the people wept....Neither be ye sorry; for the joy of the LORD is your strength"* (Nehemiah 8:9–10).

"The joy of the LORD is your strength"! This was God's answer for Israel then; and it is God's answer for us today.

The joy of the Lord is not just a side-product the Lord gives to us. It is in actuality the joy of the Lord. It is not a selfish attribute to want to be full of the joy of the Lord. Christ Himself *"who for the joy that was set before him endured the cross, despising the shame, and is set down at the right hand of the throne of God"* (Hebrew 12:2).

DON GOSSETT

GOD'S CURE FOR YOUR CARE

The Bible is a book of cures for all diseases. In fact, the great salvation which Jesus provided offers a cure for everything the devil has ever done to you.

First of all, let me say that there are diseases of the spirit as well as of the body. Many of these spiritual diseases can, if not cured early, lead to physical illnesses. Listed below are some of these spiritual "diseases" and the scriptural "prescription" for them.

Worry. Multitudes of people go through life needlessly worrying. Worry can't help you. Worry never solved a problem, paid a bill, or healed a sickness. Jesus asked, *"Which of you by taking thought* [that is, anxious though, care, or worry] *can add one cubit unto his stature?"* (Matthew 6:27). In other words, what will you gain by worrying? Jesus said, *"Take no thought for your life, what ye shall eat, or what ye shall drink; nor yet for your body, what ye shall put on. Is not the life more than meat, and the body than raiment?"* (Matthew 6:25). Then He gave the sure cure for worry: *"Seek ye first the kingdom of God, and his righteousness; and all these things shall be added unto you"* (Matthew 6:33). When your heart is fixed upon the things of the Spirit, you can be confident in the fact that God will supply all your needs.

Guilt. Are you burdened down with feelings of guilt? Are you carrying a load of sin? If your life is filled with sin, if your heart is not right with God, there is a cure for that, too. *"The blood of Jesus Christ his Son cleanseth us from all sin....If we confess our sins, he is faithful and just to forgive us our sins, and to cleanse us from all unrighteousness"* (1 John 1:7, 9). *"Blessed is he whose transgression is forgiven, whose sin is covered"* (Psalm 32:1).

Confess your sins today and accept Christ's forgiveness for your life. Then you can live a life free from the condemnation and guilt of sin.

Nervousness. If you suffer from nervousness, you are greatly hindered from enjoying life to the fullest. You are not walking in the joy that God has for you.

Do you fret over problems? Do certain persons or situations cause you anxiety which produces nervousness? Read over and over again Psalm 91, which begins, *"He that dwelleth in the secret place of the most High shall abide under the shadow of the Almighty"* (Psalm 91:1). You won't be nervous and upset if you learn how to dwell in God's secret place. As you learn to live in the presence of God, you will enjoy His perfect joy. *"In thy presence is fulness of joy; at thy right hand there are pleasures for evermore"* (Psalm 16:11).

Insomnia. Are you bothered by sleeplessness? It is startling to realize the vast number of people who are robbed of sleep every night. Let me prescribe Psalm 4:8: *"I will both lay me down in peace, and sleep: for thou, Lord, only makest me dwell in safety."* Isn't that a wonderful verse? Lie down, then, and in the name of Jesus, you can go to sleep. Enjoy the rest that God has provided for you.

Another promise in His Word is found in Psalm 127:2: *"He giveth his beloved sleep."* No longer do you need to resort to sleeping pills, for you can take the Lord's sure Word for your sleep.

The "Blues." Have you ever felt "blue"? This is nothing more than a spirit of depression and despondency that grips you and causes you to be heavyhearted. The next time you feel this way, read Psalm 42:5: *"Why art thou cast down, O my soul? and why art thou disquieted in me? hope thou in God: for I shall yet praise him for the help of his countenance."* A sure cure for a case of the blues is to sing forth the praises of God.

Fear and Anxiety. I have been astonished to discover how many of God's people are oppressed by fear. When we consider what an insidious monster fear is, we must seek freedom from its destructiveness by looking to God's Word.

Fear can produce misery, defeat, bondage, and destruction. *"Fear hath torment"* (1 John 4:18). Fear produces in-kind, for Job said, *"The thing which I greatly feared is come upon me, and that which I was afraid of is come unto me."* (Job 3:25).

The Bible doesn't call your fear a mental quirk but rather defines it as a spirit. *"For God hath not given us the spirit of fear; but of power, and of love, and of a sound mind"* (2 Timothy 1:7). *"The fear of man bringeth a snare"* (Proverbs 29:25).

Confess these words with David: *"The Lord is my light and my salvation; whom shall I fear? the* LORD *is the strength of my life; of whom shall I be afraid?"* (Psalm 27:1). If you let the Lord be your life, your light, your strength, and your salvation, you need have no fear. What can hurt you if the Lord is within? Who can harm you if you follow Christ? What disease or plague can affect your life if Christ has control? Be delivered from the fear of death, the fear of disease, the fear of calamity, the fear of old age. Whatever your fear, realize that God has not given you that fawning spirit of fear. It comes from the devil, and in Jesus' name you can cast out the spirit of fear.

God indeed has the cure for all your care. Nothing can take from you the tranquility of God's blessed care and peace in your soul. Nothing can separate you from God. Nothing can cheat you from His blessings, His healing, and His deliverance, if you will believe and obey His Word.

E. W. KENYON
ARE MIRACLES FOR US TODAY?

Many believe that the day of miracles ended with the apostolic church—that is, when the apostles died. Some are bold to say that miracles ended about 67 A.D. But John did not write his gospel until 95 to 105, or around that period, and he gave us Jesus' marvelous message in regard to the use of His name. But these promises would mean nothing if it is true that the day of miracles ended with the days of the apostles.

We cannot believe that the Holy Spirit inspired John to write the gospel of John when it would have no application to the church. We believe that miracles belong to the church as long as it is a church.

Here are some facts about miracles: Every new birth is a miracle and a greater miracle than the healing of any disease. Every answered prayer—a divine response to man—is a miracle. Miracles are divine interventions, temporarily setting aside the laws of nature.

In our ministry, miracles are the order of the day. We have seen cancers healed, sometimes instantaneously, as well as ulcers, tumors, goiters, tuberculosis, heart disease, and other diseases, too numerous to mention. If there is pain, it leaves. If there is a fever, it leaves the body. These are miracles. There have even been old chronic cases where people who have suffered for years are healed. These are miracles.

When Jesus told Peter to come that night when He was walking upon the sea, it was His invitation to walk the waves with Him. Likewise, He invites every believer into the realm of the supernatural to walk the waves with Him.

DON GOSSETT
HOW YOU CAN BE HEALED

Now that we have discussed God's cure for "spiritual" diseases, let us see what His Word has to say about healing physical diseases.

In the first place, is it truly His will that we receive healing for our bodies? His will is expressed in His Word where we read: *"Beloved, I wish above all things that thou mayest prosper and be in health, even as thy soul prospereth"* (3 John 1:2). Our loving Father expresses His wishes for us in this dynamic verse. He desires that we may prosper and be in health, even as our soul prospers. The most important thing of course is to make sure that we are prospering in our soul. This is a prerequisite to healing. The healing of our body begins with the healing of our soul.

Soul prosperity means confessing and forsaking every known sin. *"If I regard iniquity in my heart, the Lord will not hear me"* (Psalm 66:18). *"He that covereth his sins shall not prosper: but whoso confesseth and forsaketh them shall have mercy"* (Proverbs 28:13).

We read in Isaiah 59:1–2:

> *Behold, the LORD's hand is not shortened, that it cannot save; neither his ear heavy, that it cannot hear: But your iniquities have separated between you and your God, and your sins have hid his face from you, that he will not hear.*

Sometimes we may fail to receive healing, not because of the shortness of the Lord's hand nor the heaviness of His ear, but because sin has caused a break in fellowship with Him. If so, obey His Word which says, *"If we confess our sins, he is faithful and just to forgive us our sins, and to cleanse us from all unrighteousness"* (1 John 1:9). Then you will be on the right basis to believe God for healing.

Since healing begins within, let us consider another Scripture.

> *When ye stand praying, forgive, if ye have ought against any: that your Father also which is in heaven may forgive you your trespasses.*

But if ye do not forgive, neither will your Father which is in heaven forgive your trespasses. (Mark 11:25–26)

Before your prayers for healing will be effective, you must be sure that you hold no grudge or unforgiving spirit against anyone. Ask yourself, Have I allowed a hurt to cause resentment within my heart? Do I perhaps unknowingly harbor ill will against anyone? If so, your prayers for healing will not be answered. Call upon God and depend upon His unfailing grace to enable you to forgive every offense committed against you.

Healing begins within with a spiritual cleansing.

Search me, O God, and know my heart: try me, and know my thoughts: And see if there be any wicked way in me, and lead me in the way everlasting. (Psalm 139:23–24)

Who can understand his errors? cleanse thou me from secret faults. Keep back thy servant also from presumptuous sins; let them not have dominion over me: then shall I be upright, and I shall be innocent from the great transgression. Let the words of my mouth, and the meditation of my heart, be acceptable in thy sight, O Lord, my strength, and my redeemer. (Psalm 19:12–14)

It may be that a wrong confession is causing your downfall spiritually and physically. You can resolve with David, *"I will take heed to my ways, that I sin not with my tongue"* (Psalm 39:1).

It may be that your words need cleansing because your heart needs cleansing. Jesus said, *"Out of the abundance of the heart the mouth speaketh"* (Matthew 12:34). Seek from the Lord a clean heart, and then your words will be pure and edifying, ministering grace to the hearers. (See Ephesians 4:29.)

The words that we speak are of extreme importance in determining whether we enjoy healing and health or sickness and disease. Jesus said, *"He shall have whatsoever he saith"* (Mark 11:23). If we are always talking about our aches and pains, then aches and pains will be what we have. But if we talk about the goodness of the Lord, praising Him for His healing power, we can enjoy divine health.

Our tongue determines whether we have health or sickness. *"The tongue of the wise is health"* (Proverbs 12:18). If we discipline our tongue to confess, "By His stripes I am healed" (see Isaiah 53:5), then our tongue is the instrument of health.

"Pleasant words are as an honeycomb, sweet to the soul, and health to the bones" (Proverbs 16:24). Pleasant words—words pleasing to God—minister health to the believer.

"Death and life are in the power of the tongue" (Proverbs 18:21). The tongue can produce death. How? *"Thou art snared with the words of thy mouth, thou art taken [captive] with the words of thy mouth"* (Proverbs 6:2). If you speak words about sickness rather than about God's healing power, then your lips are the snare of your soul. (See Proverbs 18:7.)

"A wholesome tongue is a tree of life" (Proverbs 15:4). We know that the *"tree of life"* shall be for *"the healing of the nations"* (Revelations 22:2).

"The tongue of the wise useth knowledge aright" (Proverbs 15:2). We have full knowledge of the Scriptures which teach healing. Therefore, with our tongue, we affirm them. *"Bless the LORD…who healeth all thy diseases"* (Psalm 103:2–3). With our tongue we shall ever speak God's healing words, *"for they are…health to all their flesh"* (Proverbs 4:22).

Healing is based on the finished work of Jesus at Calvary.

He was wounded for our transgressions, he was bruised for our iniquities: the chastisement of our peace was upon him; and with his stripes we are healed.   (Isaiah 53:5)

When the even was come, they brought unto him many that were possessed with devils: and he cast out the spirits with his word, and healed all that were sick: That it might be fulfilled which was spoken by Esaias the prophet, saying, Himself took our infirmities, and bare our sicknesses.   (Matthew 8:16–17)

Jesus purchased our healing at the price of great suffering. Tradition tells us that the whip with which He was beaten was an ugly weapon. Tiny pieces of metal were woven into each of the nine leather thongs. The Roman scourging with this deadly whip surpassed all other methods of cruel punishment. It was far worse than crucifixion itself. It was so frightful that the condemned often died while being beaten with this instrument of torture.

Our Savior's hands were tied high above His head while a burly Roman soldier cruelly lashed Him with the whip. Thirty-nine times its jagged thongs gouged His tender flesh. It is said that His ribs and the bones of His back were exposed to view. In those 39 lashes, which cut His back to ribbons, our Lord bore all of our misery, pains, and sicknesses. He suffered the agony of every known disease so that we need not suffer. It was through these stripes that healing became ours.

David Bush, a missionary to Japan, was stricken with a disease that was threatening his life. While bedfast in intense pain, he read my booklet, *The Stripes that Heal*. As he read these truths, he claimed his healing. The next morning, he got up from his bed, completely well.

Our authority for healing is based on what Christ has done, and we can claim this in the name of Jesus. Know the value of your confession of faith. Declare boldly, "By His stripes I am healed." Then begin to do the things you couldn't do before. Don't waver in your faith or you will receive nothing from the Lord. (See James 1:6–8.) Resist the devil in the name of Jesus. Continue to praise the Lord with all your heart, thanking Him for healing you.

E. W. KENYON
REST IN JEHOVAH

Rest, in this sense, means quietness. A quiet spirit, a restful spirit, a faithful spirit can do business. In order for followers of Christ to be effective, they must grow quiet and restful in their spirit.

Rest in the LORD [Jehovah], and wait patiently for him: fret not thyself because of him who prospereth in his way. (Psalm 37:7)

Pay no attention to anyone else or anything else. Just rest in the Lord.

I waited patiently for the LORD; and he inclined unto me, and heard my cry. (Psalm 40:1)

Here is quiet confidence. You rest in His word. You know how to rest in the doctor, and you rest in the bank. Now I want you to rest in Jehovah. I want Jehovah to become your rest and your confidence. *"Blessed is the man that trusteth in the LORD, and whose hope the LORD is"* (Jeremiah 17:7). That is rest.

Now I am learning to rest in the Word. He said, *"My God shall supply all your need according to his riches in glory by Christ Jesus"* (Philippians 4:19). I rest fearlessly in this promise. Psalm 46:1 says, *"God is our refuge and strength, a very present help in trouble."* I rest in that Word; I depend on it. And Proverbs 3:5 says, *"Trust in the LORD with all thine heart; and lean not unto thine own understanding."*

Do not rest in anything but the Lord. He cannot fail you. Heaven and earth can pass away, but His Word cannot be broken or fail. He will never fail you.

PRAISE YOUR WAY TO HEALING

Healing is the gift of God. It is not something to be earned or deserved. First Corinthians 12:9 includes *"gifts of healing"* among the nine gifts of the Spirit. God has put the gifts of healing in the church. No one can take these gifts away.

Healing is ours because it is a provision of Christ's atonement. *"He was wounded for our transgressions, he was bruised for our iniquities: the chastisement of our peace was upon him; and with his stripes we are healed"* (Isaiah 53:5). Therefore, it is scriptural to claim that we were healed more than 2,000 years ago because *"Jesus Christ the same yesterday, and to day, and for ever"* (Hebrews 13:8). Healing is a finished work, paid for by Christ at Calvary.

Healing is a gift which is appropriated by faith. Jesus often said to those to whom He ministered, *"Thy faith hath made thee whole."* It is faith that ministers healing. The language of faith is praise.

Many people lack confidence that they can reach God. They may have confidence in the faith and prayers of others, but no assurance in their own faith and prayers.

William F. Burton, a missionary to the Congo, was filled with cancer and was completely healed as he affirmed, "Thank You, Jesus, by Your stripes I am healed." Rosa Smith, a missionary in China, had ugly pustules of small-pox all over her body. The Lord gave her a vision of an empty basket. He told her to fill it up with praises and she would be healed. She praised until the basket was filled, then went to sleep and woke up completely healed. Another lady, Connie, whose miraculous healing was reported in the newspaper, said, "I simply praised the Lord until my feet were completely healed."

Major mistakes people make in seeking healing are begging God over and over to do it, or trying to obtain enough faith even though Romans 12:3 says that *"God hath dealt to every man the measure of faith."*

We obtain healing by accepting the Word of God as the will of God and acting upon it by praising Him. Remember, our salvation and healing are already provided for. It does no good to beg God to do what He clearly has already done. We don't have to pray for Jesus to be scourged again. He has completed the work. *"By whose stripes ye were healed"* (1 Peter 2:24). All we need to do is to receive it by faith.

DON GOSSETT

THEREFORE BE BOLD

Because of who we are in Christ, there is abundant reason for living boldly, for being confident, courageous, and daring. What is there to be gained by being fearful, timid, or inferior? "Be bold, and great forces will come to your aid," said a wise man in times past. On our *Bold Bible Living* broadcasts, we do not theorize vaguely about bold living. But, like Paul of New Testament times, *"we use great plainness of speech"* (1 Corinthians 3:12). We use the Word of God in clear and ringing challenge: Therefore, be bold! In Christ you have boldness; therefore, use it! *"Having therefore, brethren, boldness to enter into the holiest by the blood of Jesus"* (Hebrews 10:19).

The Bible records in Acts 4:29, 31,

> Lord…grant unto thy servants, that with all boldness they may speak thy word….And they were all filled with the Holy Ghost, and they spake the word of God with boldness.

The element of boldness in the Christian is no accident. Nor is it something to be worked up by self-effort. It is an inherent part of the Christian. Christ has inoculated us with this daring, courageous quality—therefore, be bold in being bold!

Use what Christ has put in you. There is no room in the Christian life for the conventional, shy, barely-able-to-keep-head-above-water existence that some believe represents the Christian. Read the Word of God, especially the four Gospels and the book of Acts, and you will see that Christ's unceasing appeal to His disciples was to translate the spiritual into daring action.

E. W. KENYON
NEW BEGINNINGS

Another year has slipped into the night of the past. I wonder how much of it is lost to me, how much I can draw out of it to help in the hard places of the coming years? Of late, I have seen that the past is either a bank on which I may draw comfort, strength, and joy; or it is a harsh collector of rents long due, indulgences, or on misspent time and energy.

Is it wise to look back on the ruins of the past, to weep over the charred remains of failures? I feel it is not; yet I do it. But I have found that as we do it, the heart grows warm, the eyes are blurred, the blood flows faster, as we live again in the old fields of joy or woe.

Some of you who read this have passed through sorrow's doors and have walked with bowed heads and tear-filled eyes down the long isle with measured steps. Others have passed through joy's portals, the aisles have been flower-strewn. Another has fought battles that none but God and the tempter saw. Others have made sacrifices that have filled heaven with fragrance, earth with blessings, while their own brave hearts have wept and sung alone. Some have buried more than mortal love, have seen one light after another go out, until like the miner in the bowels of the earth whose lamp has failed, they have stumbled on in darkness, looking for the Light. Hopes have died before the blossoms kissed the sun. The thorns of bitterness have been kept close trimmed, that others might not suffer. Lines are seen that only night-sorrows cause. I fear not the griefs that walk by day; but woe to him whom dumb grief visits by night.

But all is not sorrow; joy has come to many. Love has built her nest in many a desolate heart. The song of hope is heard where the gloom was deepest. The year has had successes big with joy; new songs have been written by hearts too full of bliss to run in old molds. Wedding bells have rung. Babes have been born. The thrill of the first kiss has come—the first long, lingering embrace, the newfound joys of holy love. Yes, the old year has buried within its silent folds many an ugly scar. Healed wounds that we felt only the grace could cure. This old tear-wet year has been a friend in spite of all!

True, lovers have quarreled; hearts have been death-smitten; lives have been blighted; homes have been broken; bodies mangled; futures cursed. Yet where envy has destroyed, love has reared more magnificent mansions. Flowers grow where only rankest weeds once grew. Tears have flowed, yes, but they gave mute vent to the over pressure of the inner life. They are sorrow's safety valve, griefs sweet relief, blessed tears.

You say there have been failures. Yes, but some do not know that failures have always been used in mixing the paints that make the great masterpieces. Failures are the hidden girders that hold great lives in place. Too bad that so little is known of the great values that are oft wrapped up in the by-products of failure. Many of man's greatest achievements are failure's successes. Columbus' mistake was his success. The despairing miner who threw his pick against a rock in anger uncovered a vein of gold. So it has been in all the ages. Sorrow has done for the singer what training could not do. The blasted hope has oft revealed within its opened heart something greater. The goldsmith, looking over his misspent youth, weeps in humiliation. Then genius dips her pen in the dark, inky past and writes a masterpiece.

It takes flower and ferns years to make coal. It takes sorrows, failure, and tears to make a man appreciate his friends. Then let our flowers perish, our hopes die unborn, our ambitions fall wingless to the earth, our lights grow dim, if out of the darkness a "paradise lost" may be given to the world. Let prisons claim us, jailors chain us, if a "pilgrim's progress" may be born.

Why are we seeking painless births? Genius is mostly born of Dame Failure, in a garret, in cruel agony. When the crash comes, and one lies bleeding amid the ruins of the work of years, when hope turns down the light and ambitions fails to awaken the broken spirit, then truly great souls cry, "Thank God! I am at last identified with the great throbbing human heart."

Failure lifts the true soul into purer light. Success leads the real man to feel for the one who fails.

As I sit and look back over the year, I cry, "Old Year, you have left scars and unhealed wounds, but I love you.

"The bookkeeper, Time, has much charged against me, on some of the bills it may be hard to pay even the interest, yet I am glad that I have lived the short twelve months in your domain.

"You have had some joys that were unexpected, kept close hidden until one day you opened the door, and full-feathered they flew to me, then sang a song that has made even sorrow a joy and failure sweet.

"Goodbye, Old Year, my tears have made rivers flow across your face. There have been days with no sun, nights with no stars, deserts with no oasis, riverbeds with no water, couches with no rest, yet I love you."

But as I look back, there are mountain peaks that catch the sun and throw it back upon the clouds and fill all the past with radiance that no artist's brush could paint. I hear ripples of laughter pealing from the joyful days of the past. I hear music, it is the chimes of the bells of the past. There is no discord; distance has mellowed every note. I weep tonight, but it is not out of sorrow. I turn my heart and face the newborn year, asking, "Can you give me as much?"

DON GOSSETT

WE MAY BOLDLY SAY THAT HEALING IS OURS

Because He hath said, *"Beloved, I wish above all things that thou mayest prosper and be in health, even as thy soul prospereth"* (3 John 1:2), we may boldly say, "I have a right to prosperity and health because I am prospering in my soul."

Because He hath said, *"Himself took our infirmities, and bare our sicknesses"* (Matthew 8:17), we may boldly say, "I am free from sicknesses and disease because they were all carried by Jesus Christ for me."

Because He hath said, *"He that raised up Christ from the dead shall also quicken your mortal bodies by his Spirit that dwelleth in you"* (Romans 8:11), we may boldly say, "God is quickening my mortal body now by the very same Spirit that raised Jesus from the dead because His Spirit dwells in me; thus, I am free from weakness and sickness."

Because He hath said, *"They shall lay hands on the sick, and they shall recover"* (Mark 16:18), we may boldly say when we lay hands on the sick, "They are recovering because I am acting on His Word."

Because He hath said, *"Ye shall serve the LORD your God, and he shall bless thy bread, and thy water; and I will take sickness away from the midst of thee"* (Exodus 23:25), we may boldly say, "Sickness is taken away from me, my bread and water are blessed because I am serving the Lord my God."

Because He hath said, *"Unto you that fear my name shall the Sun of righteousness arise with healing in his wings"* (Malachi 4:2), we may boldly say, "The Lord is arising with healing for me now because I fear His name."

Because He hath said, *"He sent his word, and healed them"* (Psalm 107:20), we may boldly say, "Healing is mine now; the Lord is healing me through His Word because I have received His Word into my life."

PART IV:
WORDS THAT BRING VICTORY

NOTHING SHALL BE
IMPOSSIBLE FOR YOU

Now we are standing in the presence of Omnipotence. We are standing where God and humanity touch. We are now where man is to take over the strength of God as God took over the weakness of man.

Here we are laboring together with Christ, He sharing our burdens, we sharing His strength. He came to our level to lift us to His own, and He has done it. We are now so utterly united with Him, so a part of Him that Paul could say, *"Nevertheless I live; yet not I, but Christ liveth in me"* (Galatians 2:20).

It is not a problem of faith but a problem of privilege. Jesus has given us a legal right to the use of His name, and He had all the authority on heaven and on earth. Therefore, we have the power of attorney to use His name. *"Whatsoever ye shall ask in my name, that will I do, that the Father may be glorified in the Son"* (John 14:13). Jesus wished that the Father would be glorified in Himself, and so He challenges us to use His name. This is the miracle name, the wonderful name of Jesus. Can't you see the limitlessness of this life with Him? Can't you see that He truly meant it when He said, *"If two of you shall agree on earth as touching any thing that they shall ask, it shall be done for them of my Father which is in heaven"* (Matthew 18:19)?

Prayer becomes a cooperation with Deity. It is not begging or soliciting. It is fellowship. It is carrying out the Father's will. We have taken the place of Jesus to evangelize the world and to make the church see its wonderful privileges in Christ. Can't you see our ministry? Can't you feel the throb of the heart of God as you read this? Now you can see why nothing is impossible to you. That financial problem is not as large as it was; that disease not as formidable; that trouble is not as unconquerable! Can't you hear Him whispering, *"Fear thou not; for I am with thee"* (Isaiah 41:10)?

DON GOSSETT

WALKING WITH GOD BY AGREEING WITH GOD

We cannot truly walk with God unless we agree with Him. *"Can two walk together, except they be agreed?"* (Amos 3:3). To agree with God is to say the same thing God says in His Word about salvation, healing, prayer, and living an overcoming life.

First of all, we agree with God by saying that we are who God says we are: His child, a new creature in Christ. We say also that we are more than a conqueror through Christ. (See Romans 8:37.) We disagree with the devil who would try to convince us that we are "no good," a failure or a weakling.

How can we walk with God in power, blessing, and usefulness? By agreeing with God that we have what He says we have: His name, His nature, His power, His authority, and His love. We agree that we have what God says that we have in His Word.

Just as Enoch walked with God (see Genesis 5:22), so we can walk with God by agreeing that we have received the ability to do what He says we can do: witness with power, cast out demons, minister His healing power. *"I can do all things through Christ which strengtheneth me"* (Philippians 4:13). We agree that we can do what God says in His Word that we can do.

If we speak only what our senses dictate, we will not be in agreement with God. It is through speaking *"the word only"* (Matthew 8:8) that we agree with God. It is the "confession of faith" that is our victory.

To walk with God, we must disagree with the devil. Jesus did. By boldly declaring, *"It is written...."* He resisted the devil. You can, too. You can walk with God daily by agreeing with God and His Word. Because He has said it, so may we boldly say it. (See Hebrews 13:5–6.)

THE BOOK OF MIRACLES

The Bible is a record of miracles. Its story of creation is a series of reason-staggering miracles. Every great achievement, every step in advance recorded in the Bible for the human race has been a miracle.

As the Israelites walked in the presence of miracles, they were progressing and building up their nation. When they resorted to reason, they fell prey to their enemies and were carried into captivity. But as long as Israel walked in fellowship with God and kept their miracle covenant, they remained independent, a leader among the nations of the earth.

JESUS, A MIRACLE

Jesus, the incarnate One, was conceived in a miraculous way. His birth was accompanied by miracles. His whole life was a series of miracles, climaxing in the miracle of the ages, the death of Deity on the cross, His resurrection from the dead, and His ascension in the presence of five hundred witnesses. Jesus was a miracle from any angle. He was a greater miracle than any miracle He performed, for He was the miracle of God manifested in the flesh.

You say it is not reasonable. I know it is not. Miracles are not reasonable, but they happen. They are above reason. They belong to the realm of God. They belong to the realm of your spirit and mine. They are above the realm of reason. The church was born in a miracle; it was fostered and developed and anchored in the heathen world by miracle.

When philosophy took the place of miracles, Christianity became a religion. Wherever faith dominates, miracles take place. Wherever a body of people begin to walk with God, believe the Word and obey it, miracles follow. They must follow. You cannot have God in your midst without His manifesting Himself, and His manifestation is a miracle. Wherever an individual or a company of people dare to honor the Lord and walk with Him, miracles take place.

DON GOSSETT
TEN THINGS YOU CAN DO

Many people limit themselves unnecessarily when they say two little words: "I can't." God's Word tells us that we can do all things through Christ. (See Philippians 4:13.)

1. You can **have the desires of your heart.** *"Delight thyself also in the Lord; and he shall give thee the desires of thine heart"* (Psalm 37:4).

2. You can **witness in power.** *"Ye shall receive power, after that the Holy Ghost is come upon you: and ye shall be witnesses unto me"* (Acts 1:8). You can witness with boldness, for you have the Holy Spirit in your life.

3. You can **love others.** Jesus told us, *"Love one another; as I have loved you"* (John 13:34). Just as Jesus manifested His love for us, so we can show His love to others, for His love is shed abroad in our hearts. (See Romans 5:5.) We love with His love.

4. You can **cast out demons.** Jesus said that signs would follow those who believe on Him. *"In my name shall they cast out...they shall lay hands on the sick, and they shall recover"* (Mark 16:17–18). You have power to cast out demons and minister healing to the sick in the name of Jesus.

5. You can **do all things through Christ.** *"I can do all things through Christ which strengtheneth me"* (Philippians 4:13). You can do what God says you can do.

6. You can **have divine wisdom.** *"But of him are ye in Christ Jesus, who of God is made unto us wisdom"* (1 Corinthians 1:30). *"If any of you lack wisdom, let him ask of God, that giveth to all men liberally, and upbraideth not; and it shall be given him"* (James 1:5). You can have divine wisdom in every crisis and for every decision, for Christ Himself is your wisdom.

7. You can **possess healing and health.** *"My son, attend to my words; incline thine ear unto my sayings. Let them not depart from thine eyes; keep them in the midst of thine heart. For they are life unto those that find*

them, and health to all their flesh" (Proverbs 4:20–22). *"By* [His] *stripes ye were healed"* (1 Peter 2:24). Health and healing can be yours as you claim that which Jesus purchased for you.

8. You can **have boldness.** *"The righteous are bold as a lion"* (Proverbs 28:1). You can be as bold as a lion, for you have been made righteous with His righteousness. (See Romans 10:10; 2 Corinthians 5:21.)

9. You can **do great exploits of faith.** *"The people that do know their God shall be strong, and do exploits"* (Daniel 11:32). You can do great exploits through God who makes you strong.

10. You can **enjoy all things that pertain both to life and godliness.** *"According as his divine power hath given unto us all things that pertain unto life and godliness"* (2 Peter 1:3).

E. W. KENYON
MIRACLES BY FAITH

A miracle is a divine intervention. It is God's moving into the realm of reason and acting beneficently toward humanity. In other words, it is love moving into the reason realm and leaving a blessing behind it.

Our modern educators deny the reality of miracles. Why? Because they live in the reason realm, and their own mental processes declare that reason is the only force that can be recognized in life today. They little realize that faith has always been the lamp that has guided reason into all its achievements. They fail to recognize the fact that faith is the only creator, the only creating and dominating force in the world today.

Reason has never yet, unaided by faith, achieved one single notable victory in human progress. It was faith that built the great "Leviathan" that plies the sea. (See Job 41:1.) It was faith that drove the cable across the ocean to England when failure and reason hovered over it continually, full of dark forebodings. It was faith that gave us the wireless. It is faith that has given us everything in the mechanical, educational, and architectural arts, as well as in the literary world and musical world. Faith is the patron of all arts of civilization. Lindbergh's indomitable faith made him the outstanding man in our nation. Do you see, men and women, what faith is?

DON GOSSETT
YOU CAN DEFEAT THE DEVIL

When you are attacked by "the devil's D's" of defeat—discouragement, destruction, desolation, distress, and despair—grab your *"shield of faith, wherewith ye shall be able to quench all the fiery darts of the wicked"* (Ephesians 6:16). But don't stay on the defensive. The next step is to reach for your *"the sword of the Spirit, which is the word of God"* (Ephesians 6:17) and *"fight the good fight of faith"* (1 Timothy 6:12). Here are some Scriptures that will help you defeat his demoniacal devices!

> *He delivereth the poor in his affliction, and openeth their ears in oppression.* (Job 36:15)

> *The LORD also will be a refuge for the oppressed, a refuge in times of trouble.* (Psalm 9:9)

> *There shall no strange god be in thee.* (Psalm 81:9)

> *Let the redeemed of the LORD say so, whom he hath redeemed from the hand of the enemy.* (Psalm 107:2)

> *For ever, O LORD, thy word is settled in heaven.* (Psalm 119:89)

> *Be surety for thy servant for good: let not the proud oppress me.* (Psalm 119:122)

> *Order my steps in thy word: and let not any iniquity have dominion over me.* (Psalm 119:133)

> *If the Son therefore shall make you free, ye shall be free indeed.* (John 8:36)

> *How God anointed Jesus of Nazareth with the Holy Ghost and with power: who went about doing good, and healing all that were oppressed of the devil; for God was with him.* (Acts 10:38)

(For the weapons of our warfare are not carnal, but mighty through God to the pulling down of strong holds;) casting down imaginations, and every high thing that exalteth itself against the knowledge of God, and bringing into captivity every thought to the obedience of Christ.

(2 Corinthians 10:4–5)

They overcame him by the blood of the Lamb, and by the word of their testimony; and they loved not their lives unto the death.

(Revelation 12:11)

E. W. KENYON
DELIGHT THYSELF IN THE LORD

The faith-filled heart is a joyful heart. The doubt-filled hart is a sorrowing heart. Success comes to the smiling face. No one cares to trade with a grouchy, disagreeable personality. Only necessity drives you there. But the glad, warm hand is the hand I want. Psalm 37:4 says, *"Delight thyself also in the Lord; and he shall give thee the desires of thine heart."* The secret of answered prayer may live in praise, in joyful praise.

I prayed for one the other day, and after I was through praying, they looked so discouraged and blue that I asked, "Has He heard your prayer?"

They answered, "I suppose so."

I said, "He has not, for He only hears the prayers of the one who delights in Him."

Don't allow desperation to take the place of faith, or vague, indifferent hope to rob you of faith. Second Chronicles 32:1 says,

After these things, and the establishment thereof, Sennacherib king of Assyria came, and entered into Judah, and encamped against the fenced cities, and thought to win them for himself.

To prove your faithfulness, there will be testings. The enemy will seek your cities. But listen to the encouragement of Hezekiah, who set captains over the people and gathered them together, saying,

Be strong and of good courage, be not afraid nor dismayed for the king of Assyria, nor for the multitude that is with him; for there is a greater with us than with him; with him is an arm of flesh; but with us in Jehovah our god to help us, and to fight our battles.

DON GOSSETT

THE POWER OF THE POSITIVE PRAISE LIFE

A defeated Christian is one who does not praise the Lord. A church with a defeated spirit has no joyful praise unto God. Praise and defeat cannot live in the same house.

To practice a positive praise life requires willpower and boldness, for the natural man doesn't want to praise the Lord. The further a person is from God, the less his desire to praise Him. Worldly Christians do not enjoy the power and blessing of a positive praise life. Neither do people who are bound by sin, fear, timidity, or reluctance. Discipline your lips to praise the Lord. It is a wonderful, spiritual exercise. You will possess tremendous power, enjoy good health, and keep heaven "busy" working on your behalf.

The Bible is filled with many examples of how God blessed His people in response to their praises. We read in 2 Chronicles 5:13–14 how God moved when the people of Israel lifted their voices in praise and thanksgiving to Him at the dedication of the temple built by Solomon.

> *It came even to pass, as the trumpeters and singers were as one, to make one sound to be heard in praising and thanking the* LORD; *and when they lifted up their voice…and praised the* LORD…*that then the house was filled with a cloud, even the house of the* LORD; *so that the priests could not stand to minister by reason of the cloud: for the glory of the* LORD *had filled the house of God.*

The twentieth chapter of 2 Chronicles tells how God defeated the enemies of Israel when His people armed themselves with praise to God.

The early church was *"continually in the temple, praising and blessing God"* (Luke 24:53), and, as a result, their lives were permeated with the power of the Holy Spirit. As they continued in the power of the Holy Spirit, praising and blessing God, they multiplied rapidly, *"praising God, and having favour with all the people. And the Lord added to the church daily such as should be saved*" (Acts 2:47). Praising God produced Holy Spirit power to convict and convert sinners to Christ.

A lady named Martha from Houston, Texas, shared this testimony:

About a year and half ago, I ordered your book, *There's Dynamite in Praise*. What a book! Anointed! I couldn't stop praising the Lord. I taught your Praise Power Principles in a class where I minister. I've been diligent and have memorized almost all the 100 praise Scriptures you have written out in your book. I'm just amazed what the Lord has done for me.

You can praise your way to a life of victory and power. Praise is the password to blessing.

E. W. KENYON
HOW FAITH IS BUILT

Now *faith is the substance of things hoped for"* (Hebrews 11:1). We give substance to hope when we act on the Word. Hope is always in the future; faith is now. Believing is acting on the Word. The Word and God are one, and He is in His Word. The Word was once in Him. The Word lost none of its ability or power by being put into our language.

James says, *"Be ye doers of the word, and not hearers only, deceiving your own selves"* (James 1:22). A "doer" is a "liver." The Word lives in me in the measure that I do it. Doing the Word then is living the Word. This means God is actually living in me. I live in the Word in the measure that it functions in my daily life.

Jesus said, *"If ye abide in me* [that is, if you are a new creation], *and my words abide in you"* (1 John 15:7), then prayer becomes a simple problem. Why? Because the Word on my lips will be God's Word. God is speaking back to Himself through my lips. God, through my lips, can ask what He will, and it will be given unto me. His Word becomes a living thing on my lips, just as it was a living thing on Jesus' lips.

At Lazarus' tomb, Jesus said, *"Father, I thank thee that thou hast heard me"* (John 11:41). When the Word abides in you as it lived in Jesus, you can say the same thing to the Father. That Word can live in us and abide in us as it lived in Jesus.

We remember that when we took Christ, we received eternal life. That brought us into the family where we are to assume the place of sons and daughters. We are to take our place and assume our responsibilities as though we were children of God. We are not trying to be children, we are His children. We are not trying to get faith, because all things belong to us since we are in the family.

We are doing the Father's will as Jesus did, and the Father is backing us up as He backed up Jesus. We must study to become acquainted with the Father. *"That they might know thee the only true God, and Jesus Christ, whom thou hast sent"* (John 17:3). Did you notice what you just read? That you might know the Father, that you might know Jesus!

You may know Him through the four Gospels in a measure. You may get to know Him more fully in the Pauline Revelation, but you really get to know Him when you begin to practice the Word. When you become a "doer" of the Word, then you really get to know Him. When you pray with sick folks; when you learn to discredit senseless evidence that would contradict the Word; when you study the Word as though it were the Father's present message to you; when you talk with Him; when you fellowship with Him as you would with a loved one living with you—then you will know the Father.

DON GOSSETT

THE YOKE-BREAKER

The anointing of the Holy Spirit is given to us to loose every yoke of bondage that Satan may try to put upon us. *"The yoke shall be destroyed because of the anointing"* (Isaiah 10:27).

Jesus announced at the beginning of His ministry:

The Spirit of the Lord is upon me, because he hath anointed me to preach the gospel to the poor; he hath sent me to heal the broken-hearted, to preach deliverance to the captives, and recovering of sight to the blind, to set at liberty them that are bruised, to preach the acceptable year of the Lord. (Luke 4:18–19)

It was the anointing of the Holy Spirit in Jesus' life that enabled Him to be the liberator of Satan's captives. This same anointing has been given to us that we might minister deliverance to every captive of fear, sickness, and condemnation.

This, then, is the key to the ministry of the believer: To have the power of the Holy Spirit dwelling in our lives at all times, ready to do battle with demonic forces.

Do you have trouble reading and understanding the Word of God? Ask the Holy Spirit to illuminate those words to your mind so that they will become living words, meaningful and applicable to your life. When the Word of God becomes real to you, you will hunger for more. You will be impelled to study and know Its truths. Then you will know what your rights and responsibilities are as a believer.

Then ask the Holy Spirit to reveal to you what are the problem areas in your life and how to use your newfound power to overcome them.

For we wrestle not against flesh and blood, but against principalities, against powers, against the rulers of the darkness of this world, against spiritual wickedness in high places. Wherefore take unto you the whole armour of God, that ye may be able to withstand in the evil day, and having done all, to stand. (Ephesians 6:12–13)

The yoke-breaker is the Holy Spirit, and His tools in your life are the girdle of truth, the breastplate of righteousness, the shoes of preparation, the shield of faith, the helmet of salvation, and the sword of the Spirit, which is the Word of God. (See Ephesians 6:14–17.)

THE RADIANT LIFE

Life is full of dark shadows. Most of us are haunted by the hidden sorrows, lost or broken ideals, or early dreams stillborn in the memory. The call of other days, ignorant or mistaken, casts its unhappy shadow athwart the life. The breaking down at some crisis or failure to respond to the Spirit at a critical time causes tears and heartaches, so that laughter must be artificial and joy transient, if at all. Behind every bout of laughter is a hidden tear. Behind every bout of happiness is the ghost of other sorrows, to turn it into mourning.

Our humorists and comedians are necessary to the world. To many, their humor has taken the sharp edge from a day's disappointment. We are glad for them. The world hasn't any joy of its own, and its happiness is artificial. Likewise, the "funny sheet" and the joke column in our daily papers have come in answer to the tremendous world needs. Life is so strenuous and so full of heartaches that we have to employ men and women to amuse us. There is no natural joy; no interior joy to lift the human above earth's condition. There is no real fountain of joy. All we know is the comedian, the funny sheet, the funny story, the comical misfortune of someone.

But instead of contemplating these things and feeding your soul and spirit upon the husks of past failures, unkind acts of others, and your losses, feed and meditate upon Jesus, and you will grow to look like Him, and your life will become rich and beautiful. Your face will become radiant and full of joy; and what a blessing you will be to those about you!

The Greek word for *unto* can really be translated "into," and this opens up a vast area of helpfulness. "Looking into Jesus." Looking into that heart of love. Looking into that heart of grace and compassion and tenderness. I believe that if you should look into that heart, you would see your own face there. You would see yourself, for you have been hidden with Christ in God, and you are in Him, hidden in Him. He is your life and strength. In Him you will see yourself—the glorified, the beautiful, the victoriously, transcendently happy one. When you look into yourself, you see that all the failures and mistakes of the years are gone.

Just look into Him—contemplate Him; consider Him. What He is, you are. Don't ever look at your failures again. Don't let your environments reach their unclean hands up and drag you down to their level. Look away to Jesus! Meditate on Him. He will transform your very face from glory to glory. (See 2 Corinthians 3:18.)

Matthew 17:7–8 is a part of the transfiguration story. It tells us how Jesus was at prayer, and while He prayed, He was transfigured. Then there appeared unto Him Moses and Elijah, talking with Him. They heard the Father saying, *"This is my beloved Son, in whom I am well pleased; hear ye him"* (Matthew 17:5). The disciples fell on their faces, and I don't wonder why. When they again lifted their heads and opened their eyes, they saw Jesus only. His face was like the face of an angel; the glory of God was upon Him.

"They saw no man, save Jesus only" (Matthew 17:8). Oh, how these hearts of ours need to be shut in with Him, so that we will lose our "earth vision" and lose the outlines of our limitations, the sorrows and the mountain peaks of our failures, and in their place see Jesus only! Oh reader, if you can go alone out of the confusion that surrounds your heart and life and talk with Him until your spirit comes into fellowship with Him, until the eyes of your heart can see Jesus only, then do not hesitate!

As I speak to you today, Jesus is drawing near—Jesus with the thorn-scarred brow and the pierced heart; Jesus of Calvary; Jesus of the resurrection; Jesus of Olivet; Jesus seated at the right hand of the Majesty on high. That Jesus, our Jesus, will unveil His heart to you, unveil Himself to you, and you will have an opportunity to press your tear-stained cheek to His own. Friend, this is the only thing in these dark unhappy hours of life that will bring you comfort and strength to meet the daily demands upon you.

Read Psalms 34:5: *"They looked unto him, and were lightened: and their faces were not ashamed."* They looked unto Him and were radiant. It is a law, written deep in the human heart, that as you contemplate Jesus, if you look away into Him, you will look like Him. You cannot stand in His presence long without the fragrance of His personality impregnating your being. You can't stay long in His presence without bearing His image. You cannot hear His voice without it taking the nervous quality out of your voice and replacing it with the quality of love. You can't live with Him and He with you without His masterful grace-nature and love-nature over-shadowing and permeating your very being.

They looked unto Him and they were radiant; and they shall never be confounded. Can't you see that this is victory, that this is the law of the overcomer? I want you to look at another Scripture that has become exceedingly precious:

> *Then thou shalt see, and flow together, and thine heart shall fear, and be enlarged.*   (Isaiah 60:5)

This is a look that has life in it. We need to be enlarged. We need to be radiant to advertise the Master.

DON GOSSETT
OVERCOMING EVIL

I shall not have a wrong confession or a bad confession. A wrong confession is giving place to Satan. I have stopped talking defeat, sickness, and weakness. Defeat is of the devil. Weakness is of the devil. As long as I am speaking about these things, I am praising Satan's works and not God's!

Because He hath said, *"Resist the devil, and he will flee from you"* (James 4:7), we may boldly say, "The devil is fleeing from me because I am steadfastly resisting him in Jesus' name."

Because He hath said, *"Ye shall know the truth, and the truth shall make you free"* (John 8:32), we may boldly say, "I am set free because I know His blessed truth."

Because He hath said, *"In my name shall they cast out devils"* (Mark 16:17), we may boldly say, "Devils are going out because I have commanded them to go in Jesus' name."

Because He hath said, *"The Lord shall deliver me from every evil work"* (2 Timothy 4:18), we may boldly say, "I will not fall into any of the devil's evil snares; the Lord delivers me."

Because He hath said, *"The angel of the LORD encampeth round about them that fear him, and delivereth them"* (Psalm 34:7), we may boldly say, "The angel of the Lord encamp around me to deliver me and to protect me because I fear the Lord."

Now that you have all these Scripture verses before you, practice agreeing with God. Accept what He says for your own victorious, bold Christian walk. Believe you are what He says you are. Believe you can do what He says you can do. Believe God is what He says He is and that He will do and *is doing* what He says in His Word.

Think of yourself as God thinks of you. Remember that because *"He hath said...we* may boldly say!" Now walk in your bold living victory!

E. W. KENYON

THE ABUNDANCE OF GOD

The very title rather startles one's heart. Think of having the abundance of God for our daily walk in the presence of the Father, in place of the poverty of spirit, the lack of faith, and the lack of ability to carry out the Father's will that everyone talks to frequently about.

Let us take a look at John 10:10: *"I am come that they might have life, and that they might have it more abundantly."* Jesus declares that the reason He came to earth was that man might have an abundance of the life of God. Why? Well, it was because Satan had stripped man utterly of everything that was beautiful. And Jesus came to replenish, to rebuild, to recreate, to make man new, but especially to fill him with something that would utterly meet every need of his life.

Now, God is love, so when this abundance of life comes, there is going to come with it an abundance of love. Can you imagine what a people would be where there was an abundance of *agape*, the Jesus kind of love, so that every man and woman would be seeking to help one another? Can you imagine a church that was empty? Love would go out hunting for needy folks. Every car would be crowded with folks that were spiritually poverty-stricken.

My heart was touched by this Scripture: *"Ye are of God, little children"* (1 John 4:4). You are born out of abundance, born out of fullness; you are of God. You are the sons and daughters of God. You are of God, and nothing will so enrich the life as for us to quietly say, "I am of God. I am begotten of God. I have God's very nature in me." Along with His nature, you have His ability to help folks, a burden-bearer, a strength-giver, an inspiration to men. Men and women will say of you, "That man is a faith-builder."

He touches your very innermost being and floods you with His natural ability and grace and love. *"Ye are of God, little children, and have overcome them"* (1 John 4:4). The man of God is masterful; he is a conqueror. *"Beloved, let us love one another: for love is of God; and every one that loveth is born of God, and knoweth God. He that loveth not knoweth not God; for God is love"* (1 John 4:7–8). You have become a partaker of the love nature of the Creator. You are tied up with Omnipotence. You are tied up with the very effulgence of God. You have His strength, His grace, His ability. You have Him. You are not seeking a blessing from Him; you have the blessing in you! Think what it would mean for you to have the consciousness of His presence in you all the time.

When you awaken in the morning, you will say, "Good morning, Father. You are going to be with me today. You are going to give me confidence in every crisis. You are going to be grace to me for every need all through the day."

Wonderful, isn't it? Is there anything you cannot do with Him abiding in you? God's very life abides in you. Colossians 2:9–10 says, *"In him dwelleth all the fulness of the Godhead bodily. And ye are complete in him, which is the head of all principality and power."* Carefully note it now, *"In* [Jesus] *dwelleth all the fulness of the Godhead bodily."* All the ability of God was in Him. All the love of God was in Him. He never gave anyone the sense of emptiness, lack of ability, or a sense of unreadiness. He was always ready to meet every emergency.

I think of His utter completeness, fullness, and ability in every place. We are made full with His fullness. It is a complete garment, a full garment; it does not skimp anywhere. It did not come to you because you fasted and prayed to get it. It came to you all through grace.

When Paul was persecuting Jesus, Jesus said to him, *"Saul, Saul, why persecutest thou me?"* (Acts 9:4). When Paul bruised a person, a single branch, he was also bruising the Vine. Never was it more beautiful and more clear than when Jesus said, *"I am the vine, ye are the branches"* (John 15:5). Hear the Master say, "Saul, you have been bruising, cutting, and mangling the branches; you have hurt the Vine."

When Jesus wanted someone to have His revelation, He did not choose John or James, but He took Saul of Tarsus and unveiled to him the most marvelous thing ever put into human language: the Pauline Revelation. It was not given to a worthy man; it was given to a man whose heart was dominated by hatred, envy, and bitterness. The Father took this man and filled him with His fullness. It is all of grace. Everyone can be full with His fullness. Of His fullness have we all received. We have received the fullness of His love, His life, the fullness of everything that was beautiful in the man Jesus.

Ephesians 3:7 says, "*Whereof I was made a minister, according to the gift of the grace of God given unto me by the effectual working of his power.*" Let us look carefully at this verse: "*Whereof I was made a minister.*" It was according to the gift of the grace of God—that unmerited, wonderful thing. Grace is a gift. It was gift of gifts; it was love overflowing.

Now you can understand how Christ could say, "I am come that you might have life, might have God, might have an abundance of God, according to the gift of grace which was given me according to the working of His power in me." (See John 10:10.)

I want you to notice that Jesus continually made confession of what He was, what the Father was to Him, and what He was to the Father. Now Paul is following in the footsteps of the Master, and he is making a confession, "I was made a master according to the gift of His grace." (See Ephesians 3:7.) What is His grace? It is "*according to the riches of his glory*" (Ephesians 3:16). I have been let into the secret place, where I have discovered the wealth, the undeveloped riches of His heart.

In Colossians chapter 2, He says this: "*In whom are hid all the treasures of wisdom and knowledge*" (Colossians 2:3). Wisdom is the most important thing in the world. You can know the Bible so that men will be amazed at your knowledge, but you may be unable to use that knowledge to instruct or help others. You may know the Bible from Genesis to Revelation but not have the wisdom to feed the people, to build them up. If you want to get the best things, you must go and dig for it. The choicest diamonds are deep; the richest pearls are deep. The genius of God hiding everything was this: In delving, you develop your intellect, you develop your spirit, and you develop yourself in the work, and after a while, you come to appreciate Him. As you study the Word, you will run across things you never knew about. You will find treasures.

You are just like the mighty Columbia River. For thousands of years that water has been flowing down, and then along came someone and put in the Grand Coulee Dam and harnessed that tremendous force. You have had the omnipotence of God flowing through and around you, and you have the ability to heal sick folks in Jesus' name; to set men and women free that were held in bondage. But you have not used it. If you let the ability of God work in you, hundreds of lives might be changed. You may make those desert lives blossom like a rose. The unused and untapped resources of God are in every one of us.

Ephesians 3:16 says, *"That he would grant you, according to the riches of his glory, to be strengthened with might by his Spirit in the inner man."* The transcendent glory and beauty of God's grace is going to dawn upon our spirits, and we are going to taste of the riches of His glory, and we are going to experience the joy of being strengthened with His ability in our spirits. Your whole being will be rooted and grounded in love...in Him. You have received the abundance of grace. When you receive eternal life, you receive the gift of righteousness, the abundance of grace. You have the nature of the Father—His ability, His steadfastness, His gentle kindness. He imparts His very confidence to you and makes you strong and courageous.

So get into the habit of saying, "He is in me; He lives in me; His love is in me."

THE JOY-FILLED LIFE

Outside of the Christian life, I have found limited happiness and pleasure. For instance, being an athlete and achieving some honors brought a measure of happiness. Being elected the president of my high school student body was indeed a satisfying experience. And there have been other facets of life that have brought pleasure.

However, it has been my experience, along with many others, to discover that the life of "Christ within" is the real joy-filled life. I am convinced that joy is only found in the Christian life, for this joy is something Jesus brought to the earth. The angel sang, *"Behold, I bring you good tidings of great joy, which shall be to all people…a Saviour, which is Christ the Lord"* (Luke 2:10–11). And Jesus gave us joyful words just before He returned to heaven, *"These things have I spoken unto you, that my joy might remain in you, and that your joy might be full"* (John 15:11).

Yes, it is this joy that makes the Christian's life different from people of the world. *"The joy of the LORD is your strength"* (Nehemiah 8:10). And this joy holds the Christian steadfast in times of stress. He can rejoice when all others are miserable.

James said, *"My brethren, count it all joy when ye fall into divers temptations; knowing this, that the trying of your faith worketh patience"* (James 1:2–3). Jesus taught, *"Blessed are ye, when men shall revile you, and persecute you, and shall say all manner of evil against you falsely, for my sake. Rejoice, and be exceeding glad: for great is your reward in heaven"* (Matthew 5:11–12).

The disciples rejoiced because they were accounted worthy to suffer shame for Christ's name. (See Acts 5:40.) Paul and Silas sang praises to God in the most uncomfortable of circumstances. (See Acts 16:23–25.) Paul could say he was always rejoicing even when sorrowful. (See 2 Corinthians 6:10.) Even in these troublesome times, the Christian finds that the joy of the Lord is with him to sustain him.

E. W. KENYON
COUNT IT DONE

Count done in you and for you what the Word declares. Rise up and meet the Word halfway. Embrace the Word with joy. Whatever the Word says about you is God's picture of you. When He says that He has "*delivered us from the power of darkness*" (Colossians 1:13)—that is, Satan's power—then you have been delivered out of it. You have been translated into the kingdom of the Son of His love—that is, in the family of God. Satan has no legal right to reign over you. Jesus is the Lord and head of the body of Christ. God has delivered you. You play the part of the delivered one. He delivered you out of the hand of the adversary. Satan has no right to put disease on you. He cannot hem you in with want and lack so that you cannot meet your obligations. He simply cannot do it. I know that to be true, that God is unto us a God of deliverance.

Not only does He deliver us out of financial and physical needs, but His grace can reach the deepest need of man. I know that He is able to make all grace abound unto us, that we, having all things, may abound in every good work. The fullness of His ability is ours. The fullness of His comfort is ours. The fullness of His grace and love is ours.

You dare to say, "I am today redeemed, delivered from the dominion of my enemy, the devil; stand complete in Christ. I am the righteousness of God in Him." Say it with your lips until your heart says it. Somehow, your spirit is dependent upon your speech. Say with the psalmist, "*The Lord is my light and my salvation; whom shall I fear?*" (Psalm 27:1). God is our righteousness. He is our ability today. We have a legal right to use the name of Jesus, which has enwrapped within it the ability to conquer every difficulty.

Then we want to confess boldly what He has done in us, and not only what He has done for us, but what He has made us to be. Scriptures says, "*Therefore if any man be in Christ, he is a new creature: old things are passed away*" (2 Corinthians 5:17). The old things of failure, of want, and of weakness are things of the past. We stand complete in Him. We are reconciled. There is nothing between you and Him. You and He are one. He is on your side.

His love is shed abroad in you. God is love (see 1 John 4:8), and when He sheds abroad His love in our hearts, He is shedding abroad in us Himself, His very nature. You have become a partaker of it. You have it in you. Now you are going to give it sway.

You are going to let Him do as He pleases in you, as He did in Jesus. What the Word says we are, our hearts acknowledge. We are the very sons and daughters of God. We are partakers of His divine nature. We are more than conquerors. We have the mind of Christ in His Word, so that we may know His will, and we can live in it.

There is no compromise in God. There should be no compromise in our confession. When He says, "Of his fulness have all we received" (John 1:16), we ought to say, "Thank you, Father." What He has done for us must not be annulled by our negative confession, and our confession must be the Word. We overcome the adversary by the Word that is in our testimony. We say, "Upon the cross with Him I died, and I was buried with Him, too. I was made alive and justified."

DON GOSSETT

NINE STEPS FOR VICTORY

Baptism is an outward sign of an inward work of grace. Now that you have been born again, you should be baptized in water according to the command of Jesus. Some people have been baptized as infants, before they were saved. One pastor I know says this: "Baptism is the immersion in water of a saved person. If you weren't saved when you got baptized, you didn't get baptized—you just got wet!" If you are truly serious about your salvation, you will be baptized in water as soon as possible. Jesus said, *"He that believeth and is baptized shall be saved; but he that believeth not shall be damned"* (Mark 16:16).

Bible reading is the food your spirit feeds on. Peter wrote, *"As newborn babes, desire the sincere milk of the word, that ye may grow thereby"* (1 Peter 2:2).

Prayer is simply talking to God. When you talk to Him, expect Him to answer you, and when you make requests of Him, expect Him to meet your needs. Jesus said, *"Verily, verily, I say unto you, Whatsoever ye shall ask the Father in my name, he will give it you"* (John 16:23). You can find God's will revealed in the Bible:

> *This is the confidence that we have in him, that, if we ask any thing according to his will, he heareth us: And if we know that he hear us, whatsoever we ask, we know that we have the petitions that we desired of him.* (1 John 5:14–15)

Fellowship with other Christians is important for your spiritual growth. *"And let us consider one another to provoke unto love and to good works: Not forsaking the assembling of ourselves together, as the manner of some is; but exhorting one another"* (Hebrews 10:24–25). I would go so far as to say that nobody in the world can live a good Christian life without keeping good company. Bad company ruined Samson and Solomon. It caused Peter to swear and to deny his Lord. Be like the psalmist who said, *"I was glad when they said unto me, Let us go into the house of the LORD"* (Psalm 122:1).

Resist temptation in order to walk in victory. *"There hath no temptation taken you but such as is common to man: but God is faithful, who will not suffer* *you to be tempted above that ye are able; but will with the temptation also make a way to escape, that ye may be able to bear it"* (1 Corinthians 10:13). Remember that it is not a sin to be tempted to do wrong; it is a sin only when you yield to that temptation. Trust Jesus to give you daily victory and cleansing through His precious blood. *"If we confess our sins, he is faithful and just to forgive us our sins, and to cleanse us from all unrighteousness"* (1 John 1:9).

Praising the Lord is one of the greatest secrets of achieving constant spiritual victory. Praise will work wonders in your life. Your life will be a witness to others of God's goodness and will glorify the great and wonderful God whom you love and serve. *"Whoso offereth praise glorifieth me"* (Psalm 50:23).

The baptism of the Holy Spirit is absolutely essential if you want to live in the realm of the miraculous. Be sure to attend a church that believes in the baptism of the Holy Spirit with the evidence of speaking in tongues. Praying in tongues will build up your faith (see Jude 1:20); it will help you pray according to the will of God (see Romans 8:26–27); and it will give you your own special language with which your spirit can communicate with God (see 1 Corinthians 14:2). In addition, you need this endowment of power to possess the ability of God in all activities of your Christian life.

Soul winning is the Christian activity closest to Jesus' heart; and as His follower, you must be more concerned about winning souls than about anything else you do. Pray daily for the lost, witness and testify to the Lord's saving grace in your own life at every opportunity, and give to soul-winning ministries.

Tithes and offerings will keep your finances in good shape. (See Malachi 3:8–12; Luke 6:38.) A tithe is 10 percent of your earnings; God owns the first 10 percent of anything you earn. On the other hand, offerings are love gifts you give to God in addition to your tithe.

Finally, if doubts should come concerning your salvation, rely on the Word of God for your assurance. Remember, God cannot lie; it is the devil who is a liar and a thief. Satan would like to deceive you and steal the blessings of God away from you, but he can do nothing unless you let him. Daily present yourself—spirit, soul, and body—as a vessel of honor for the Lord's service. Tell him, "Lord, I will go where you want me to go; I will do what you want me to do," and the devil will have to flee. *"Submit yourselves therefore to God. Resist the devil, and he will flee from you. Draw nigh to God, and he will draw nigh to you"* (James 4:7–8).

E. W. KENYON

SEIZING OPPORTUNITIES

An opportunity is a free ride into town. An opportunity is a job that is going to challenge me to win. An opportunity is a chance to get my feet on the first rung of the ladder, a chance for me to get into my place in the sun.

I am alert and ready. I got up early. I shaved, bathed, did my morning exercises. I breathed deeply. I meditated awhile, sat alone with Him, and breathed in His courage and strength. Then I went out on the wayside and waited for my opportunity. I saw it coming. I was dressed. I was fit. I had been trained. I leaped aboard. I swung into action.

I was ready when my opportunity came.

I remember that Paul, who became God's mouthpiece and gave to the world the greatest exposition—the greatest unveiling of the man of Galilee that was ever known—said, "Buy up your opportunities." (See Colossians 4:5.)

It would be a great inspiration if you and I could find why God chose Paul to be His mouthpiece, why He chose him to write the epistles that he wrote and give that intimate unveiling of what Jesus did during those fifty wonderful days, from the time He was nailed to the cross until He sat down on the right hand of the Majesty on high. I imagine it was because Paul was ready. He was likely more ready than any other man living in his generation. He had been putting something into his preparation that challenged God.

I will be ready when He comes, not ready for the call to leave my body but ready to minister as never before. It is not what I get out of it. It is what I am able to get from Him and give to the world. It is a big thing.

I say to you, Be ready, for in such a moment as you think not, your greatest opportunity will come. So study, train, get in shape. The opportunity will come. There will be room for you in this opportunity to make your place in life.

Paul was not lucky. He was a worker. He got ready. When his opportunity came, he seized it and swung into action. He is a winner because he planned to win.

VICTORY OVER PRIDE

Pride is a spirit—an evil one. As such, the best way to fight it is with *"the sword of the Spirit, which is the word of God"* (Ephesians 6:17). This is the same weapon Jesus fought with when He was tempted by the devil in the wilderness, and we can use it exactly the same way He did. When the devil comes against you in this area, simply say, "Devil, it is written…," followed by one or more Scriptures that are appropriate to the situation. Here are a few to start you off:

> *The LORD shall cut off all flattering lips, and the tongue that speaketh proud things: Who have said, With our tongue will we prevail; our lips are our own: who is lord over us?* (Psalm 12:3–4)

> *Thou wilt save the afflicted people; but wilt bring down high looks.* (Psalm 18:27)

> *Him that hath an high look and a proud heart will not I suffer.* (Psalm 101:5)

> *Thou hast rebuked the proud that are cursed, which do err from thy commandments.* (Psalm 119:21)

> *Though the LORD be high, yet hath he respect unto the lowly: but the proud he knoweth afar off.* (Psalm 138:6)

> *Surely he scorneth the scorners: but he giveth grace unto the lowly.* (Proverbs 3:34)

> *When pride cometh, then cometh shame: but with the lowly is wisdom.* (Proverbs 11:2)

> *Only by pride cometh contention.* (Proverbs 13:10)

He that despiseth his neighbour sinneth.   (Proverbs 14:21)

Every one that is proud in heart is an abomination to the LORD: *though hand join in hand, he shall not be unpunished.*
(Proverbs 16:5)

Pride goeth before destruction, and an haughty spirit before a fall.
(Proverbs 16:18)

Let another man praise thee, and not thine own mouth; a stranger, and not thine own lips.   (Proverbs 27:2)

Thus saith the LORD, *Let not the wise man glory in his wisdom, neither let the mighty man glory in his might, let not the rich man glory in his riches: but let him that glorieth glory in this, that he understandeth and knoweth me, that I am the* LORD *which exercise lovingkindness, judgment, and righteousness, in the earth: for in these things I delight, saith the* LORD.   (Jeremiah 9:23–24)

Because thou hast trusted in thy works and in thy treasures, thou shalt also be taken.   (Jeremiah 48:7)

Behold, this was the iniquity of thy sister Sodom, pride, fulness of bread, and abundance of idleness was in her and in her daughters, neither did she strengthen the hand of the poor and needy.
(Ezekiel 16:49)

Woe unto you, Pharisees! for ye love the uppermost seats in the synagogues, and greetings in the markets.   (Luke 11:43)

Charity suffereth long, and is kind; charity envieth not; charity vaunteth not itself, is not puffed up.   (1 Corinthians 13:4)

If a man think himself to be something, when he is nothing, he deceiveth himself.   (Galatians 6:3)

Let nothing be done through strife or vainglory; but in lowliness of mind let each esteem other better than themselves. (Philippians 2:3)

Wherefore he saith, God resisteth the proud, but giveth grace unto the humble. (James 4:6)

All that is in the world, the lust of the flesh, and the lust of the eyes, and the pride of life, is not of the Father, but is of the world. (1 John 2:16)

Because thou sayest, I am rich, and increased with goods, and have need of nothing; and knowest not that thou art wretched, and miserable, and poor, and blind, and naked: I counsel thee to buy of me gold tried in the fire, that thou mayest be rich; and white raiment, that thou mayest be clothed, and that the shame of thy nakedness do not appear; and anoint thine eyes with eyesalve, that thou mayest see. (Revelation 3:17–18)

For victory over pride, pray, "Dear Father, I ask you for freedom from every spirit of pride. I never want you to have to resist me. In Jesus' name, I choose to walk humbly."

E. W. KENYON
SALESMANSHIP

Real salesmanship is the highest order of evangelism. It is the very science of propaganda. It is achieved by a double sale. Every propagandist, every salesman, every evangelist sells himself before he sells his commodity. If his commodity is a part of himself, he has sold his commodity when he has sold himself. If he is better than his commodity, the buyer "buys" him and takes the commodity on the side. In discussing salesmanship, we cannot discuss the commodity; we can only discuss the "seller."

The secret of salesmanship is to hide behind the great thing you are selling, so that, after awhile, the prospective customer stops seeing you and sees instead the things you are selling. No matter what the article you are selling is, you must make it so desirable and so attractive that the prospective buyer wants it more than they want anything else. If the demand isn't there when you meet them, you must create the demand, and that demand must overrule every objection.

What are the steps that will lead to a demand for your article, you ask? In the first place, it must be an honest article. It must be a worthwhile article. It must be a needed article. We, as personal workers, know that our Christ, whom we are "selling" to the world, is the most honest, worthwhile, needed article to man.

Before we go to convince people of this, we should be so utterly "sold" on it ourselves, so that when people look at us, they can see whom we represent. They can see that He is a part of us, that we are a part of Him. Then we must overcome prejudices created by past personal workers, or "salesmen" as we shall call them.

The first requisite is genuineness. You can't be an actor and put it over. If a worker who has the false things can act a part so well that he can make people believe it and compel them to take it when it is false and worthless, then his place is not in personal work but in Hollywood. Acting is not necessary. It is not true salesmanship. You have come with a genuine answer to their problem.

Second, your ambition is to give the public something that they need, something that is worthwhile. There flows out from your personality something that puts a fragrance in your words and arrests their attention immediately. They are tired, busy, and prejudiced, but the fragrance of your earnestness and genuineness is a blessing to them. They listen to you. If you hold in your mind only the thought of what you will get out of this contact, they will feel it in your spirit; they will hear it in your tones. But if you know it will be to their profit and their benefit, they will feel this in you.

So, sell yourself first. Sell them the biggest and most real personality, a spirit of loyalty to the big things of life, and before you ever reach their side, they will feel it.

The small tricky spirit receives its reward; the lofty, noble, spirit receives its reward. Let us cultivate the very character and life and spirit of the Man of the ages.

SHARING WITH JESUS

What a thrill there is in being tied up with Christ, in fellowship with Omnipotence, having a share in the work of redemption of the human race.

Go ye therefore, and teach all nations, baptizing them in the name of the Father, and of the Son, and of the Holy Ghost: Teaching them to observe all things whatsoever I have commanded you: and, lo, I am with you alway, even unto the end of the world.

(Matthew 28:19–20)

This Great Commission is a revelation of our sharing with Him. (See also Mark 16:16–20.)

You see, He became identified with us in our lost state. Now we have become identified with Him, seated upon the throne. We really have a throne life and throne ability to represent Him. This means carrying the gospel to every creature; not only do we carry it across the water in heathen lands but we also carry it to the men and women who live on the same block as us.

Remember how Christ shared Himself with us? He became one with us. He assumed our sins, our weaknesses, and our diseases. He became utterly one with us in His effort to redeem us. Now we are to become one with Him to carry out His dream for the world. He died for us; we live for Him. He died for them; we live for them.

Sin is becoming very powerful in the world. The saloon business and the cigarette habit and the roadhouses are taking the young people from our churches. They are holding in bondage a vast army of slaves, and you and I are personally responsible for their slavery. We have the ability to set them free, to bring them the message of emancipation.

Handing a dollar to a hobo is not carrying out the Great Commission. Rather, it is intelligently putting the money where it will do the most good. There are urgent calls for us to help the starving of the whole world, but that is not leading them to Christ. I feel that our first ministry must be for their salvation. I would not ignore their physical needs in any way, but I believe that first things come first. They need the Bread of Life even more than they need corn and wheat.

But think of the wasted abilities that could be harnessed for God if you started taking advantage of your opportunities. You have the equipment, the living Word, the mighty Spirit, and the name of Jesus. God is your ability. Jesus is made wisdom unto you. All you need to do now is to show yourself approved unto God, a workman that need not be ashamed, handling with divine wisdom this living Word among the people. Don't put it off any longer.

Many of you who read this are under condemnation because you have lived such selfish lives. Remember that it is only a little while before you meet the Master, and what will you say?

I wonder if you have ever led a soul to Christ, if you have ever prayed with a sick one and seen him healed. Why, you have God's life, God's very nature within you. You have the cooperation of the Holy Spirit. You have the living Word. What more could you ask for? Arise, and go speak to that young man!

DON GOSSETT

WORDS CAN WORK BLUNDERS

Words work wonders, but they can also work blunders!

Did you realize that multitudes of people fail in life because they talk failure, they fear failure, they really believe in failure?

What you say locates you. You will not—you cannot—rise above your own words. If you talk defeat, failure, anxiety, sickness, and unbelief, you will live on that level. Neither you nor anyone else, no matter how clever, will ever live above the standard of your conversation. This spiritual principle is unalterable. If your conversation is foolish, trifling, impractical or disorganized, your life is invariably the same way. With your words, you constantly paint a *public* picture of your *inner self*. Jesus said, *"Out of the abundance of the heart the mouth speaketh"* (Matthew 12:34).

When you think back on your life, you will probably agree that most of your troubles have been tongue troubles. The Bible says, *"Whoso keepeth his mouth and his tongue keepeth his soul from troubles"* (Proverbs 21:23). Oh, the trouble caused by unruly tongues! Words spoken in the heat of the moment—words of anger, words of harshness, words of retaliation, words of bitterness, words of unkindness—produce trouble for us.

Beloved, let's make it our prayer right now, *"Let the words of my mouth, and the meditation of my heart, be acceptable in thy sight, O Lord, my strength, and my redeemer"* (Psalm 19:14). Here's another good Bible prayer: *"Set a watch, O Lord, before my mouth; keep the door of my lips"* (Psalm 141:3). It is really important that we let God help us overcome our unruly speech habits, for our words can work blunders and get us into much trouble.

A negative confession precedes possession of wrong things. The Bible warns, *"Thou art snared with the words of thy mouth, thou art taken with the words of thy mouth"* (Proverbs 6:2). With the mouth confession can be made, not only to the good things God has promised us, but with the mouth confession can be made unto sickness, defeat, bondage, weakness, lack, and failure.

Refuse to make a bad confession. Refuse to make a negative confession. Repudiate a dual confession where you are saying at one moment "By His stripes, I am healed" and at the next moment "But the pain is still there." Your negative confession denies the healing Scripture, and you will go on in defeat.

E. W. KENYON
"CROSS" RELIGION

I heard a missionary from South America say that he wanted to buy a little gold cross, and he hunted through all the jewelry shops of a South America city and could not find one without a dead Christ hanging on it. That dead Christ on the cross is a symbol of a religion, born of spiritually dead men.

The sinner does not find Christ on the cross; he finds Christ seated at the right hand of the Father. On the cross, He was not a Savior. He was a substitute. He was made sin on the cross.

When He cried, *"It is finished"* (John 19:30), He meant that He had finished the work He came to do under the Old Covenant. He had fulfilled the Abrahamic covenant. He had fulfilled the sacrifices. He had fulfilled the blood of atonement that had been sprinkled upon the altars for 1,500 years. The work was finished.

That Old Covenant died with Him on the cross. The Israelite nation died with Him on the cross. They didn't know it, but they nailed themselves to the cross with Christ. The covenant, the priesthood, and the nation died with Christ.

We were identified with Him on the cross, but there is no salvation in death. On that cross, "[God] *hath made him to be sin for us, who knew no sin*" (2 Corinthians 5:31).

Have you ever thought of the two unanswered prayers in the New Testament—the one in the garden, where Christ said, *"If thou be willing, remove this cup from me"* (Luke 22:42), and the other on the cross, where He said, *"My God, my God, why hast thou forsaken me?"* (Matthew 27:46). Read the Psalm 22 carefully to see how utterly Jesus was forsaken by the Father on the cross when He was made sin.

THE FIGHT OF FAITH

Recognize that until the victory is fully manifested you are engaged in a fight of faith—a struggle, a battle. A battle of believing against symptoms which would discourage you or which contradict what you believe. Too many people think that if they just had enough faith, all would be easy and everything would be fixed as though some magic wand had been waved over them. A study of faith in the Bible, however, reveals that the man of faith believes God against all kinds of odds and circumstances. His prayers are answered as a result of persistent faith because he is fully convinced that God's promises are true, regardless of circumstances. So I urge you to face the Scriptures squarely and make a decision once and for all whether what you are seeking is God's will for you. Then act on that decision.

If it's in the Word, it's yours. When you are quoting God's Word, you can be as bold as the Word. Matthew 8:17 says, "[He] *took our infirmities, and bare our sicknesses.*" That includes you. This Scripture declares that those physical burdens you carry were taken by Christ. You need not beg Him to do that which is already done. Look at this verse, memorize it, and then look up into the face of Christ, talk directly to Him, and thank Him personally for taking your diseases and weaknesses.

While you look into His face, picture Him as He was stretched to a whipping post, His back bared and bleeding as a Roman soldier plowed furrows on His body with a whip. As you remember Him there, hear the lash of the cat-o'-nine-tails as it slashes through the air and strikes His back. As you think upon the terrible suffering of our Lord, you will hear the Holy Spirit say to you, "Through the lashings of that whip and the groans of the Saviour, He suffered our pains and carried our diseases, and with His stripes we are healed."

Then you will be facing the facts of your rights in Christ. They will become real to you as you affirm that "[He] *took our infirmities, and bare our sicknesses.*" You will begin to see them as actual truths instead of just a healing theory. Don't embrace a healing theory but embrace the reality of

Jesus and what He died to provide for you. Let the Spirit of God administer the reality of that to you. For He was beaten for you. He bore your sickness; He took your weakness. The truth of this will grip you deeply as you meditate upon the provision of our Lord and what it cost Him to provide healing for you.

This is God's covenant declaring that you are already healed because Christ took your diseases. Only Satan would burden you with a disease which Christ has already borne for you. Jesus proved that He wants you to be well. (See 3 John 1:2.) But you are in the midst of a battle. Satan is opposing you, but God has provided for your deliverance. You have to claim that deliverance as your right.

You must make the decision: This sickness or oppression is of Satan, so it cannot stay. Christ took it. You are free; you are healed. It must be true, so claim it! You will not be denied.

Jesus paid for your health; it belongs to you. You need not fear this thing. It cannot destroy you because Jesus destroyed it for you. Resist the work of Satan. Jesus is in you. He has lifted your load. He is your strength, your health, your life. By His stripes you are healed—now!

I KNOW THAT I AM RIGHTEOUS

Job knew that he was righteous by the standards of righteousness in his day. It will be of vast importance to you to be able to say to your enemies, "I know that I am righteous with the righteousness of Jesus Christ. I know that I am righteous because God has declared me righteous when I confessed Jesus as my Savior and Lord. I know that I am righteous because God calls me the righteous one who lives by faith."

You have as much a right to call yourself righteous as you have to call yourself a new creation or a child of God. Paul said, *"Therefore if any man be in Christ, he is a new creature"* (2 Corinthians 5:17), or a child of God. And we do not doubt that; we say amen to that.

If you are a new creation, you are the righteousness of God in Christ. God not only declares that you are righteous, but He makes you righteous and makes your righteousness Himself. That threefold fact should fill your heart with joy and your mouth with singing.

John declared, *"Beloved, now are we the sons of God"* (1 John 3:2). You do not doubt that; you rejoice in that. So rejoice in your righteousness.

Righteousness means the ability to stand in the Father's presence without the sense of guilt or inferiority. *"What God hath cleansed, that call not thou common"* (Acts 10:15).

One of the unhappy things today many of us do is to continually condemn ourselves. We have not prayed enough; we have not done this or that. If this is the case with you, ask for His forgiveness and rise up and take your place as a son or daughter in Christ. Allow His grace to strengthen you to face every obstacle that comes your way.

Job was accused of being unrighteous, but he never yielded to his accusers. He maintained his integrity. So you, too, must stop yielding to accusations and rise up and take your place, confidence of your righteousness in Christ. Stand on the Word of God, and God will honor you, as He honored Job.

DON GOSSETT

MY NEVER AGAIN LIST

"Can two walk together, except they be agreed?"
—Amos 3:3

Let me set the facts straight: Amos 3:3 declares that if we are to walk with God in blessing, triumph, and provision, we must discipline our hearts and mouths to agree with God. When I learned this truth many years ago, I wrote "My Never Again List." I wrote these twelve affirmations out of a sense of sheer desperation. I didn't just sit down at my typewriter and compose something—I had just experienced the most humiliating event of my life: the repossession of my home and five rooms of furniture!

"Repossession"—that ugly, hateful work that hurts so deeply! I was so embarrassed over those losses. I knew the problem wasn't God or His integrity—the problem was me. What was my problem? I couldn't effectively walk with God and still agree with His Word. My words were out of harmony with God's Word! I spoke lack, fear, defeat, worries, frustrations, the devil's supremacy, and what all I cannot do! It was "resurrection day" for me when I began to activate my faith by speaking this God-given discipline, which I titled "My Never Again List." It was not just "nice words" to impress anyone; it was my sincere response to God and His truth that brought release and provision for urgent needs.

How about you, reader? If your life is in any way hemmed in with defeat, lack, fear, sickness, doubt, or bondage, please accept my challenge to daily speak out these simple twelve affirmations of God's truth! I pray that this discipline will help you as it did me—and continues to do!

MY NEVER AGAIN LIST

Never again will I confess "I can't," for *"I can do all things through Christ which strengtheneth me"* (Philippians 4:13).

Never again will I confess lack, for *"my God shall supply all* [my] *need according to his riches in glory by Christ Jesus"* (Philippians 4:19).

Never again will I confess fear, for *"God hath not given* [me] *the spirit of fear, but of power, and of love, and of a sound mind"* (2 Timothy 1:7).

Never again will I confess doubt and lack of faith, for *"God hath dealt to every man the measure of faith"* (Romans 12:3).

Never again will I confess weakness, for *"the* Lord *is the strength of my life"* (Psalm 27:1), and *"The people that do know their God shall be strong, and do exploits"* (Daniel 11:32).

Never again will I confess supremacy of Satan over my life, for *"greater is he that is in* [me], *than he that is in the world"* (1 John 4:4).

Never again will I confess defeat, for *"God always causeth* [me] *to triumph in Christ"* (2 Corinthians 2:14).

Never again will I confess lack of wisdom, for *"Christ Jesus, who of God is made unto* [me] *wisdom"* (1 Corinthians 1:30).

Never again will I confess sickness, for *"with his stripes* [I am] *healed"* (Isaiah 53:5), and Jesus *"himself took* [my] *infirmities and bare* [my] *sicknesses"* (Matthew 8:17).

Never again will I confess worries and frustrations, for I am *"casting all* [my] *cares upon him who careth for* [me]*"* (1 Peter 5:7). In Christ, I am "carefree!"

Never again will I confess bondage, for *"where the Spirit of the Lord is, there is liberty"* (2 Corinthians 3:17). My body is the temple of the Holy Spirit!

Never again will I confess condemnation, for *"there is therefore now no condemnation to them which are in Christ Jesus"* (Romans 8:1). I am in Christ; therefore, I am free from condemnation.

ABOUT THE AUTHORS

DR. E. W. KENYON

Dr. E. W. Kenyon (1867–1948) was born in Saratoga County, New York. At age nineteen, he preached his first sermon. He pastored several churches in New England and founded the Bethel Bible Institute in Spencer, Massachusetts. (The school later became the Providence Bible Institute when it was relocated to Providence, Rhode Island.) Kenyon served as an evangelist for over twenty years. In 1931, he became a pioneer in Christian radio on the Pacific Coast with his show *Kenyon's Church of the Air*, where he earned the moniker "The Faith Builder." He also began the New Covenant Baptist Church in Seattle. In addition to his pastoral and radio ministries, Kenyon wrote extensively.

DON GOSSETT

Don Gossett (1929–2014) served the Lord through full-time ministry for more than fifty years. Born again at the age of twelve, Don answered his call to the ministry just five years later and began by reaching out to his unsaved family members. Don apprenticed with many well-known evangelists, beginning with William Freeman, one of America's leading healing evangelists during the late 1940s. He also spent time with Raymond T. Richey, Jack Coe, and T. L. Osborn. Don's many writings have been translated into almost twenty languages and have exceeded twenty-five million in worldwide distribution. His daily radio show, launched in 1961, has been broadcast worldwide. Don raised five children with his first wife, Joyce, who died in 1991. In 1995, Don found lifelong love again and married Debra, an anointed teacher of the Word. They ministered worldwide and lived in British Columbia, Canada, and in Blaine, Washington State.